THE BIBLE AND HOMOSEXUALITY

THE BIBLE AND HOMOSEXUALITY

EXPANDING OUR IMAGE OF GOD

THE OUTREACH GUIDE

EDITED BY Michael J. O'Loughlin
FOREWORD BY James Martin, SJ

Paulist Press
New York / Mahwah, NJ

Cover image by YERMAKOVA HALINA/Shutterstock.com
Cover and book design by Lynn Else

Library of Congress Cataloging-in-Publication Data
Names: O'Loughlin, Michael J. (Writer in Washington, DC) editor | Martin, James, 1960– writer of foreword
Title: The Bible and homosexuality: expanding our image of God / edited by Michael J. O'Loughlin; foreword by James Martin, SJ.
Description: New York; Mahwah, NJ: Paulist Press, [2025] | Summary: "This anthology of essays by scripture scholars and religious writers discusses biblical references to homosexuality"—Provided by publisher.
Identifiers: LCCN 2025015919 (print) | LCCN 2025015920 (ebook) | ISBN 9780809157693 paperback | ISBN 9780809189359 ebook
Subjects: LCSH: Homosexuality—Biblical teaching | Bible and homosexuality
Classification: LCC BS680.H67 B49 2025 (print) | LCC BS680.H67 (ebook)
LC record available at https://lccn.loc.gov/2025015919
LC ebook record available at https://lccn.loc.gov/2025015920

ISBN 978-0-8091-5769-3 (paperback)
ISBN 978-0-8091-8935-9 (ebook)

Published by Paulist Press
997 Macarthur Boulevard
Mahwah, NJ 07430
www.paulistpress.com

Printed and bound in the
United States of America

Dedication

To those who strive to make our church welcoming

CONTENTS

CONTENTS

FOREWORD

James Martin, SJ

Encountering God in the Bible is one of the most fulfilling parts of the Christian life. Learning how God loved and led the people of Israel in the Old Testament helps us understand more fully what theologians call "salvation history." Likewise, meeting Jesus in the Gospels and experiencing his love, mercy, and compassion is often at the heart of a Christian person's faith. And reading the letters of St. Paul and other leaders in the early church encourages, consoles, and inspires us.

The Bible, then, is the treasured friend of billions of believers.

But for many LGBTQ Christians, the Bible can feel like the enemy. In the Book of Leviticus, for example, homosexuality is called an "abomination" (18:22; 20:13). And while Jesus never explicitly condemns homosexuality, though he certainly could have (he is hard on divorce, for example), St. Paul does (1 Cor 6:9–10). The very few biblical verses that address homosexuality are used against LGBTQ people over and over: in the political sphere, by religious leaders, on social media, in one-on-one encounters, and perhaps worst of all, in homilies and sermons in the very churches where LGBTQ people seek to encounter a loving God.

By the same token, the Bible prescribes many laws, moral codes, and ethical guidelines that modern-day Christians ignore, don't follow, or have rejected completely. For example, even though Christians honor the Old Testament, we don't stone people who work on the Sabbath (Exod 35:2); we don't sell people into slavery (Exod 21:7); and if someone curses God, we don't execute them (Lev 24:10–16). In the New Testament, St. Paul told slaves to be obedient to their masters (Eph 6:5–8). He also said that women should be silent in churches (1 Cor 14:34). Often, the same people who loudly quote Bible verses against homosexuality are silent about other biblical practices that any thoughtful person would reject today. So there is usually a troubling selectivity in which Bible verses "count."

Besides, Catholics are neither literalists nor fundamentalists. So one response to what are often called "clobber verses"—because people have used them to "clobber" LGBTQ people—is to see them in their historical context and to remember that even devout Christians shouldn't do everything that the Old Testament commands; likewise regarding the letters in the New Testament. The questions, though, remain: How can we best understand what the Bible says on homosexuality? What did these passages mean then and what do they mean today? And for LGBTQ Christians, there are other important questions: How can we square these verses with Jesus, who reached out to those on the margins? How can LGBTQ people, their friends, families, and allies, read these Bible verses? How can LGBTQ people respond thoughtfully and charitably when the "clobber verses" are used against them?

Outreach, an LGBTQ Catholic ministry that operates under the auspices of America Media, has assembled some of the world's most renowned biblical scholars, as well as LGBTQ advocates, to answer these questions. A few years ago we started publishing these essays on our website, outreach.faith. The response was astonishing.

The online version of the Outreach Guide to the Bible and Homosexuality quickly became by far the most popular feature of our website, to a degree that continues to astonish us. Even during weeks of "high traffic" with major news stories (say, the pope pronouncing on an LGBTQ issue) these Bible essays would still receive the most hits. Clearly, there is a hunger among LGBTQ people—and people in general—for a clearheaded look at these verses, and for a clearheaded look at the Bible in general, from some of the most respected and trustworthy scholars, writers, and believers. The same held true in our Outreach conferences: panels and talks on the Bible consistently drew the largest crowds and the most energetic questions. So naturally, we thought a small, portable book would be an excellent resource, and we are glad that Paulist Press agreed to publish it.

We hope that these essays will help LGBTQ people, their families, and their friends understand the individual passages from the Bible on homosexuality, be more able to respond when these verses are used against them, and, most importantly, feel more at home with the Bible, where God desires to encounter and embrace all of us, including LGBTQ people.

1

"TEXTS OF RIGOR" AND "TEXTS OF WELCOME"

Walter Brueggemann, PhD

It is easy to see at first glance why LGBTQ people, and those who stand in solidarity with them, look askance at the Bible. After all, the two most cited biblical texts on the subject are the following, from the old purity codes of ancient Israel:

> You shall not lie with a male as with a woman; it is an abomination. (Lev 18:22)
>
> If a man lies with a male as with a woman, both of them have committed an abomination; they shall be put to death, their blood is upon them. (Lev 20:13)

There they are. There is no way around them; there is no ambiguity in them. They are, moreover, seconded by another verse that occurs in a list of exclusions from the holy people of God: "He whose testicles are crushed or whose male member is cut off shall not enter the assembly of the LORD" (Deut 23:1). This text apparently concerns those who had willingly become eunuchs to serve in foreign courts. For those who want it simple and clear and clean, these texts will serve well. They seem, moreover, to be echoed in this famous passage from the Apostle Paul:

> And exchanged the glory of the immortal God for images resembling mortal man or birds or animals or reptiles. Therefore God gave them up in the lusts of their hearts to impurity, to the dishonoring of their bodies among themselves, because they exchanged the truth about God for a lie and worshiped and served the creature rather than the Creator, who is blessed for ever! Amen. For this reason God gave them up to dishonorable passions. Their women exchanged natural relations for unnatural, and the men likewise gave up natural relations with women and were consumed with passion for one another, men committing shameless acts with men and receiving in their own persons the due penalty for their error. (Rom 1:23–27)

Paul's intention here is not fully clear, but he wants to name the most extreme affront of the Gentiles before the Creator God, and Paul takes disordered sexual relations as the ultimate affront. This indictment is not as clear as those in the tradition of Leviticus, but it does serve as an echo of those texts. It is impossible to explain away these texts. Given these most frequently cited texts—which we may designate as *texts of rigor*—how may we understand the Bible given a cultural circumstance that is very different from that assumed by and reflected in these old traditions?

Well, start with the awareness that the Bible does not speak with a single voice on any topic. Inspired by God as it is, all sorts of persons have a say in the complexity of Scripture, and we are under mandate to listen, as best we can, to all of its voices. On the question of gender equity and inclusiveness, consider the following to be set alongside the most frequently cited texts. We may designate these texts as *texts of welcome*. Thus, the Bible permits very different voices to speak that seem to contradict those texts cited above. The prophetic poetry of Isaiah 56:3–8 has been taken to be an exact refutation of the prohibition in Deuteronomy 23:1:

> Do not let the foreigner joined to the LORD say,
> "The LORD will surely separate me from his people";
> and do not let the eunuch say,
> "I am just a dry tree."
> For thus says the LORD:
> To the eunuchs who keep my sabbaths,
> who choose the things that please me
> and hold fast my covenant,
> I will give, in my house and within my walls,
> a monument and a name
> better than sons and daughters;
> I will give them an everlasting name
> that shall not be cut off.
>
> And the foreigners who join themselves to the LORD,
> to minister to him, to love the name of the LORD,
> and to be his servants,
> all who keep the sabbath, and do not profane it,
> and hold fast my covenant—
> these I will bring to my holy mountain,
> and make them joyful in my house of prayer;

their burnt offerings and their sacrifices
  will be accepted on my altar;
for my house shall be called a house of prayer
  for all peoples.
Thus says the LORD God,
  who gathers the outcasts of Israel,
I will gather others to them
  besides those already gathered. (Isa 56:3–8)

This text issues a grand welcome to those who have been excluded, so that all are gathered by this generous, gathering God. The temple is for "all peoples," not just the ones who have kept the purity codes. Beyond this text, we may notice other texts that are tilted toward the inclusion of all persons without asking about their qualifications or measuring up the costs that have been articulated by those in control. Jesus issues a welcoming summons to all those who are weary and heavy laden:

> Come to me, all who labor and are heavy laden, and I will give you rest. Take my yoke upon you, and learn from me; for I am gentle and lowly in heart, and you will find rest for your souls. For my yoke is easy, and my burden is light. (Matt 11:28–30)

No qualification, no exclusion. Jesus is on the side of those who are "worn out." They may be worn out by being lower-class people who do all the heavy lifting, or it may be those who are worn out by the heavy demands of Torah, imposed by those who fill the Torah with judgment and exclusion.

By Jesus mentioning his "yoke," Jesus contrasts his simple requirements with the heavy demands that are imposed on the community by teachers of rigor. Jesus's quarrel is not with the Torah, but with Torah interpretation that had become, in his time, excessively demanding and restrictive. The burden of discipleship to Jesus is easy, contrasted to the more rigorous teaching of some of his contemporaries. Indeed, they had made the Torah exhausting, specializing in trivialities while disregarding the neighborly accents of justice, mercy, and faithfulness (Matt 23:23).

A text in Paul echoes a baptismal formula in which (unlike Romans 1) all are welcome without distinction: "There is neither Jew nor Greek, there is neither slave nor free, there is neither male nor female; for you are all one in Christ Jesus" (Gal 3:28). No ethnic distinctions, no class distinctions, and no gender distinctions. None of that makes any difference "in Christ," that is, in the church. We are all one, and we all may be one. Paul has become impatient with his friends in the churches in Galatia who have tried to order the church according to the rigors of an exclusionary Torah. In response, he issues a welcome that overrides all the distinctions that they may have preferred to make.

Finally, I will cite the remarkable narrative of Acts 10. The Apostle Peter has raised objections to eating food that, according to the purity codes, is unclean; thus he adheres to the rigor of the priestly codes, not unlike the ones we have seen in Leviticus. His objection, however, is countered by "a voice" that he takes to be the voice of the Lord. Three times that voice came to Peter amid his vigorous objection: "What God has cleansed, you must not call common" (Acts 10:15).

The voice contradicts the old purity codes! From this, Peter can enter new associations in the church. He declares: "You yourselves know how unlawful it is for a Jew to associate with or to visit any one of another nation; but God has shown me that I should not call any man common or unclean" (Acts 10:28). And from this Peter further deduces: "Truly I perceive that God shows no partiality, but in every nation any one who fears him and does what is right is acceptable to him" (Acts 10:34–35).

This is a remarkable moment in the life of Peter and in the life of the church, for it makes clear that the social ordering governed by Christ is beyond the bounds of the rigors of the old exclusivism. I take the texts I have cited to be a fair representation of the very different voices that sound in Scripture. It is impossible to harmonize the mandates of exclusion in Leviticus 18:22, 20:13, and Deuteronomy 23:1 with the welcome stance of Isaiah 56, Matthew 11:28–30, Galatians 3:28, and Acts 10.

Other texts might be cited as well, but these are typical and representative. As often happens in Scripture, we are left with texts in deep tension, if not in contradiction with each other. The work of reading the Bible responsibly is the process of adjudicating these texts that will not fit together.

The reason that the Bible seems to speak "in one voice" concerning matters that pertain to LGBTQ persons is that the loud voices most often cite only one set of texts, to the determined disregard of the texts that offer a counter position. But our serious reading does not allow such disregard, so we must have all the texts in our purview.

The process of the adjudication of biblical texts that do not readily fit together is the work of interpretation. I have termed it "emancipatory work," and hope to show why this is so. Every reading of the Bible—no exceptions—is an act of interpretation. There are no "innocent" or "objective" readings, no matter how sure and absolute they may sound. Everyone is engaged in interpretation, so one must pay attention to how we do interpretation. In what follows, I will identify five things I have learned concerning interpretation, thing I hope will be useful as we read the Bible responsibly around the crisis of gender identity in our culture.

THE INTERPRETER'S LIFE EXPERIENCE

All interpretation filters the text through the life experience of the interpreter. The matter is inescapable and cannot be avoided. The result, of course, is that with a little effort, one can prove anything in the Bible. It is immensely useful to recognize this filtering process. More specifically, I suggest that we can identify three layers of personhood that likely operate for us in doing interpretation.

First, we read the text according to our *vested interests*. Sometimes we are aware of our vested interests; sometimes we are not. It is not difficult to see this process at work concerning gender issues in the Bible. Second, beneath our vested interests, we read the Bible through the lens of our fears, which are sometimes powerful, even if unacknowledged. Third, beneath our vested interests and our fears, I believe we read the Bible through our hurts, which we often keep hidden not only from others but from ourselves as well. The defining power of our vested interests, our fears, and our hurts make our reading lens seem to us sure and reliable. We pretend that we do not read in this way, but it is useful that we have as much self-critical awareness as possible. Clearly, the matter is urgent for our adjudication of the texts I have cited.

It is not difficult to imagine how a certain set of vested interests, fears, and hurts might lead to an embrace of the insistences of *texts of rigor* that I have cited. Conversely, it is not difficult to see how LGBTQ persons and their allies operate with a different set of filters, and so gravitate to the *texts of welcome*.

CONTEXT

There are no texts without a context, and there are no interpreters without a context that positions them to read in a distinct way. Thus the purity codes of Leviticus reflect a social context in which a community under intense pressure sought to delineate, in a clear way, its membership, purpose, and boundaries.

The text from Isaiah 56 has as its context the intense struggle, upon return from exile, to delineate the character and quality of the restored community of Israel. One cannot read Isaiah 56 without reference to the opponents of its position in the more rigorous texts, for example, in Ezekiel. And the texts from Acts and Galatians concern a church coming to terms with the radicality of the graciousness of the gospel, a radicality rooted in Judaism that had implications for the church's rich appropriation of its Jewish inheritance.

Each of us interpreters also has a specific context. But we can say something quite general about our shared interpretive context. It is evident that Western culture—and our place in it—is at a decisive point wherein we are leaving behind many old, long-established patterns of power and meaning, and we are observing the emergence of new patterns of power and meaning. It is not difficult to see our moment as an instance anticipated by the prophetic poet: "Remember not the former things, nor consider the things of old. Behold, I am doing a new thing; now it springs forth, do you not perceive it? I will make a way in the wilderness and rivers in the desert" (Isa 43:18–19).

The "old things" among us have long been organized around white male power, with its tacit, strong assumption of heterosexuality, plus a strong accent on American domination. The "new thing" emerging among us is a multiethnic, multicultural, multiracial, multigendered culture in which old privileges and positions of power are placed in deep jeopardy. We can see how our current politico-cultural struggles (down to the local school board) have to do with resisting what is new and protecting and maintaining what is old, or, conversely, welcoming what is new with a ready abandonment of what is old.

If this formulation from Isaiah fits our circumstance in Western culture, then we can see that the *texts of welcome* are appropriate to our "new thing," while the *texts of rigor* function as a defense of what is old. In many specific ways our cultural conflicts—and the decisions we must make—reverberate with the big issue of God's coming newness.

In the rhetoric of Jesus, this new arrival may approximate among us the "coming of the kingdom of God," except that the coming kingdom is never fully here but is only "at hand," and we must not overestimate the arrival of newness. It is inescapable that we do our interpretive work in a context that is, in general ways, impacted by and shaped through this struggle for what is old and what is new.

THE ARRIVAL OF TEXTS

Texts do not come to us one at a time, *ad seriatim*, but always *in clusters through a trajectory of interpretation*. Thus, it may be correct to say that our several church denominations are, importantly, trajectories of interpretation. Location in such a trajectory is important, both because it imposes restraints upon us, and because it invites bold imagination in the context of the trajectory. We do not, mostly, do our interpretation in a vacuum. Rather we are "surrounded by so great a cloud of [nameable] witnesses" who are present with us as we do our interpretive work (Heb 12:1).

For now, I worship in a United Methodist congregation, and it is easy to see the good impact of the interpretive trajectory of Methodism. Rooted largely in Paul's witness concerning God's grace, the specific Methodist dialect, mediated through Pelagius and then Arminius, evokes an accent on the "good works" of the church community in response to God's goodness.

That tradition, of course, passed through and was shaped by the wise, knowing hands of John Wesley, and we may say that, at present, it reflects the general perspective of the World Council of Churches with its acute accent on social justice. The interpretive work of a member of this congregation is happily and inevitably informed by this lively tradition.

It is not different from other interpretive trajectories housed in other denominational settings. We are in such interpretive trajectories that allow for innovation and continuity. Each trajectory provides for its members some guardrails for interpretation that we may not run too far afield, but that also is a matter of adjudication—quite often a matter of deeply contested adjudication.

A "CRISIS OF THE OTHER"

We are, for now, deeply situated in a *crisis of the other*. We face folk who are quite unlike us, and their presence among us is inescapable. We are no longer able to live our lives in a homogenous community of culture-related "lookalikes." There are, surely, many reasons for this new social reality: global trade, easier mobility, electronic communication, and mass migration among them.

We are thus required to come to terms with the "other," who disturbs our reductionist management of life through sameness. We have a simple choice that can refer to the other as a threat, a rival enemy, and a competitor, or we may take the other as our neighbor. The facts on the ground are always complex, but the simple human realities with each other are not so complex.

While the matter is pressing and acute in our time, this is not a new challenge to us. The Bible provides ongoing evidence about the emergency of coming to terms with the other. Thus the land settlements in the Book of Joshua brought Israel face-to-face with the Canaanites, a confrontation that was mixed and tended toward violence (Judges 1).

The struggle to maintain the identity and the purity of the holy people of God was always a matter of dispute and contention. In the New Testament, the long, hard process of coming to terms with "Gentiles" was a major preoccupation of the early church, and a defining issue among the apostles. We can see in the Acts of the Apostles that over time, the early church reached a readiness to allow non-Jews into the community of faith.

And now among us the continuing arrival of many "new peoples" is an important challenge. There is no doubt that the *texts of rigor* and the *texts of welcome* offer different stances in the affirmation or negation of the other. Certainly, among the "not like us" folk are LGBTQ persons, who readily violate the old canons of conformity and sameness. Such persons are among those who easily qualify as "other," but they are no more and no less a challenge than many other "others" among us.

And so the church is always redeciding about the other, for we know that the "other"—LGBTQ persons among us—are not going to go away. Thus we are required to come to terms with them. The trajectory of the *texts of welcome* is that they are to be seen as neighbors who are welcomed to the resources of the community and invited to make contributions to the common well-being of the community. By no stretch of any imagination can it be the truth of the gospel that such "others" as LGBTQ persons are unwelcome in the community.

In that community, there are no second-class citizens. We had to learn that concerning people of color and concerning women. And now the time has come to face the same gospel reality about LGBTQ persons as others who are welcomed as first-class citizens in the community of faithfulness and justice. We learn that the other is not an unacceptable danger, and is not required to give up "otherness" to belong fully to the community. We in the community of faith, as in the Old and New Testaments, are always called to respond to the other as a neighbor who belongs with "us," even as "we" belong with and for the "other."

THE GOSPEL VERSUS THE BIBLE

The gospel is *not to be confused with or identified with the Bible*. The Bible contains all sorts of voices that are inimical to the good news of God's love, mercy, and justice. Thus, biblicism is a dangerous threat to the faith of the church because it allows into our thinking claims that are contradictory to the news of the gospel. The gospel, unlike the Bible, is unambiguous about God's deep love for all peoples. And where the Bible contradicts that news, as in the *texts of rigor*, these texts are to be seen as "beyond the pale" of gospel attentiveness.

Our interpretation is filtered through our close experience; our context calls for an embrace of God's newness; our interpretive trajectory is bent toward justice and mercy; our faith calls us to the embrace of the other; and our hope is in the God of the gospel and in no other. Thus the full acceptance and embrace of LGBTQ persons follows as a clear mandate of the gospel in our time. Claims to the contrary are contradictions of the truth of the gospel on all the counts indicated above.

These several learnings about the interpretive process help us grow in faith:

- We are warned about the subjectivity of our interpretive inclinations.
- We are invited in our context to receive and welcome God's newness.
- We can identify our interpretive trajectory as one bent toward justice and mercy.
- We may acknowledge the "other" as a neighbor.
- And we can trust the gospel in its critical stance concerning the Bible.

All these angles of interpretation, taken together, authorize a sign for LGBTQ persons: Welcome! Welcome to the neighborhood! Welcome to the gifts of the community! Welcome to the work of the community! Welcome to the continuing emancipatory work of interpretation!

2

INTERPRETING SCRIPTURE AND CHURCH TEACHING

Elizabeth A. Johnson, CSJ

With great skill, biblical scholars have forged a set of strong and supple tools to bring forth enlightened, often profound, interpretations of Scripture. They know that the Bible is inspired, but also that it did not drop down straight from heaven. So, they work out meaning by placing texts in their human settings.

What is the situation in life, the historical context, that produced this passage? What issue is being addressed? What do the words mean in the original language? What is the literary genre (for one does not interpret poetry the same way as narrative or law)? Is the text unique or like other passages? What is its relation to the main streams of biblical teaching that deal with how to live in relation to a gracious and merciful God, whom the New Testament succinctly identifies in one word: "love" (1 John 4:8)?

Especially when studying Scripture to discern where the Holy Spirit is leading the church, scholars using such tools have shed helpful light on difficult texts such as those that have been used to support slavery, promote the subordination of women, clobber LGBTQ persons, or ignite anti-Semitism. There is a great line in *Dei Verbum*, the Second Vatican Council's document on revelation, that underscores the value of this work. "It is the task of exegetes to work according to these rules toward a better understanding and explanation of the meaning of Sacred Scripture, so that through preparatory study the judgment of the Church may mature" (*DV* 12).

In other words, the church's capacity to grasp the gospel can grow, and good biblical interpretation can help make it happen. In the process, compassion and a commitment to justice, which give life to the gospel commandments of love, also grow in the church both as an official institution and as a graced community of disciples following Jesus Christ.

INTERPRETING CHURCH TEACHING

It flies beneath the radar, perhaps, but theologians today are using similar kinds of tools to interpret the wide body of church teaching. Like biblical writings, religious doctrines about beliefs and moral teachings about human behavior have come about through historical processes. With roots in Scripture, they developed over time in response to new circumstances and new questions, as the original core community of believers in the upper room at Pentecost moved out into the wider Mediterranean world, the wider European, North and South American, African, and Asian worlds—the wider global world.

Ways of thinking and what is just assumed to be the case in one culture do not necessarily translate with the same ring of truth to other times and places. In addition, as the world changes, new issues arise about which people in former eras could not have even dreamed. And always, through the ongoing spiritual experiences of people who treasure the faith, "there is growth in the understanding of the realities and words which have been handed down" (*DV* 8).

Consequently, what we call a development of doctrine can take place. The fundamental truth of the gospel can be expressed with new insight. Some teaching may even be reformed, as has happened with the profound changes in Catholic moral teaching on freedom of conscience, lending money for profit, and slavery.

As with the Bible, so too with the tradition: church teachings found in the *Catechism* and Vatican declarations need to be interpreted rather than read off in a simplistic, fundamentalist manner. The church's capacity to grasp the gospel can grow, and good theological interpretation can help make it happen.

INTERPRETING CHURCH TEACHING ON LGBTQ ISSUES

This is surely relevant to LGBTQ persons who are Catholic and to those who love and support them. In a nutshell, church teaching in their regard strongly affirms that all LGBTQ persons are created in the image of God and, as such, as the *Catechism of the Catholic Church* states, should be accepted with "respect, compassion, and sensitivity" (§ 2358). Furthermore, it accords them equal human dignity with heterosexual persons and urges that they be treated with pastoral care and compassion.

At the same time, this teaching distinguishes the homosexual orientation from bodily homosexual activity, judging the latter to be "intrinsically disordered"[1] and contrary to natural law. It holds that under no circumstances should homosexual unions be legally recognized, let alone blessed. LGBTQ persons are instructed to live a life of self-denial through sexual abstinence, joining the suffering they experience to the sacrifice of Christ's cross.

Living with integrity in a church with such teaching requires tools of interpretation to deal with what may or may not resonate with one's personal experience before others and before God. In a broader framework, these tools are also needed to discern where the Holy Spirit is leading the church and to figure out God's priorities and intentions for the world. What tools might be available to us?

THE DULLES TOOLKIT

One exceptionally helpful toolkit for discernment was assembled by the late Cardinal Avery Dulles, SJ, a leading North American theologian, in his 1982 book *The Survival of Dogma: Faith, Authority, and Dogma in a Changing World*. Tremendously concerned with encouraging people in their faith, yet worried that many in our culture found church teaching archaic or meaningless, he developed six principles that can be used to interpret official church statements. Using these tools critically and carefully, people could distinguish the good

1. Congregation for the Doctrine of the Faith, *Persona Humana*: Declaration on Certain Questions Concerning Sexual Ethics, The Holy See, December 29, 1975, sec. VIII, https://www.vatican.va/roman_curia/congregations/cfaith/documents/rc_con_cfaith_doc_19751229_persona-humana_en.html.

grain of revealed truth from the chaff of time-conditioned formulas, and so live lives better oriented toward Christ. To be clear, Dulles did not deal with Catholic teaching about LGBTQ issues. But his tools may be usefully applied by those who do. Here are his six interpretive tools with the varied examples he used to illustrate them.

In interpreting church teaching, heed should be paid to different types of literary forms. Biblical scholars have no trouble recognizing metaphor, myth, prophetic oracle, and so forth. Consequently, they do not feel obliged to take literally many statements that were previously thought to refer to miraculous divine interventions. The question of genre should also be applied to official church documents.

In the past, popes and councils often spoke in ways common to high officials of their time, using a majestic style and issuing anathemas against those who disagreed. Even now, some in authority are inclined to speak with an emphasis that treats the faithful as passive recipients of their teaching. Interpret this rhetoric according to its proper form. "If hyperbole is to be admitted in the Bible, who is to deny that it may also be found in ecclesiastical pronouncements?" writes Dulles.[2]

An antiquated worldview, presupposed but not formally taught in an earlier church teaching, should not be imposed as binding doctrine. Cosmology has changed. People in the biblical and medieval worlds assumed a three-tiered universe. The earth and its creatures sat at the center, surrounded by the heavens with God and the angels above, and the underworld with Satan and his demons below. To force this worldview today is

2. Avery Dulles, SJ, *The Survival of Dogma: Faith, Authority, and Dogma in a Changing World* (Crossroad Publishing, 1982), 176. The principles set forth by Dulles are discussed further in Elizabeth Johnson, CSJ, "Fluency of Interpretation: A Key to Avery Dulles's Practice of Theology," in *The Survival of Dulles: Reflections on a Second Century of Influence*, ed. Michael M. Canaris (Fordham University Press, 2021), 41–50.

pointless. The teaching of gospel truth needs to be framed by a contemporary scientific understanding of the world. In the process, many classical ideas about creation, miracles, and resurrection, among others, will be transformed.

Technical terms should be interpreted in terms of the structure of thought presupposed by those who used them. Philosophy has also changed. Much Christian doctrine has been phrased in categories of Greek philosophy, such as spirit and matter, substance and accident, and so on. As with cosmology, these terms need to be understood in their historical framework and not taken as literal descriptions. For example, transubstantiation makes sense as an explanation of the Eucharistic mystery if one thinks that physical realities are made up of substance and accident.

But different philosophical systems of today do not think of physical entities in these terms. This requires that the real presence of Christ in the Eucharist be spoken of in a different way.

When interpreting theological terms, pay attention not only to what they literally mean (denote), but also to the ideas and feelings they imply or stir up (connote). Truth being taught is often wrapped up in imagery and concepts that are not of the essence. For example, in announcing the good news of salvation, the New Testament declares that we have been redeemed by the blood of Christ. The image of sacrificial blood is laden with connotations from the exodus, temple worship, and Mosaic law.

Since medieval times, Christ's bloody death has been seen as a penalty paid to God to make satisfaction for sin. Today, these bloody conceptions of redemption, embedded in patriarchal and feudal culture, are unintelligible and even repugnant. Church doctrine needs to articulate the great issues of sin, salvation, and redeemed life in Christ with contemporary vocabulary.

No church teaching of the past directly solves a question that was not asked at the time.[3] In other words, whenever the state of the evidence about a question materially changes, we have a new question which cannot be answered by appealing to old authorities. For example, the sixteenth-century Council of Trent, quoting the Apostle Paul, taught that Adam was a single individual, and his actions were the source of original sin. Modern science has raised the likely scenario that humans evolved from more than one original couple.

Using Paul and Trent today to insist on monogenism is not legitimate, as Dulles put it, because neither of them was dealing with the question of the origin of humanity. In fact, the question never entered their minds. They read Genesis as history and took for granted that Adam was a single individual.

In the Bible and in authoritative doctrinal statements, one should be alert for signs of social pathology and ideology. Ever a pilgrim wending its way through history, the church must always be reforming a greater fidelity to the gospel. At times, it fails and sins. For example, fanatical teaching against the Jews who did not accept Christianity, defensive statements against Protestants, vigorous papal rejection of the modern idea of freedom: all are due to sociopathological forces at work.

To maintain authority, these forces gave rise to teaching marked by narrowness (for example, outside the church there is no salvation) and harshness toward adversaries. Gospel truth is not taught by the church in divine form, but in human form. The effects of human weakness and sinfulness can be embedded in the language of church teaching itself. We must take care to draw a line between what is a matter

3. Dulles, *The Survival of Dogma*, 179.

of faith and what is to be set aside as wrongful human judgments.

Dulles makes the case that using these principles will train us in a suppleness of mind capable of discerning the core message of the gospel. This is not an "anything goes" approach. For one thing, the subject of faith's commitment is the infinite mystery of the all-holy God made known in Christ, whose Spirit enlivens the church. This is a mystery of love beyond imagining. This mystery can never be totally captured in the net of church teaching, nor can the divine will be known in absolute terms for all circumstances. For another, historical change can raise severe challenges to faith. While sharing a common commitment across generations, our situation today is as different from that of our medieval ancestors as the computer is different from the abacus. Given both the transcendence of God and the historical conditioning of human beings, interpreting church teaching with tools of intelligent discernment is essential. It is, in Dulles's phrasing, a practice of "creative theology."[4]

THE GRAVITY OF TRADITION

For two thousand years, the Christian tradition has held that heterosexuality is the norm for human beings. Marriage is the vocation to which most heterosexual people are called. Fidelity to marriage vows is of primary importance. Considering the commandment forbidding adultery (Exod 20:14), sexual intercourse with someone other than one's marriage partner is a grave sin.

For various reasons, including the need to provide for children that may result from sexual union, church teaching—

4. Dulles, *The Survival of Dogma*, 178.

and even the *sensus fidelium* or "sense of the faithful," at least until recently—has maintained the immorality of sexual acts outside of marriage. This is a weighty tradition with backing in Scripture and theology, worthy of respect and not to be put aside lightly.

In this context, a new issue has now appeared over the horizon, namely, the standing of persons who are not heterosexual. Such persons have always existed, of course, but cultural changes are making it possible for many to "come out" to themselves and others about their own deep identity in body and spirit. What religious assessment is to be made of LGBTQ persons?

For example, are they, too, beloved creatures made in the image and likeness of God? What ethical values should govern their personal behavior, including intimate sexual activity? For example, are there principles within tradition itself that could permit sexual activity within a monogamous, permanent same-sex relationship?

These are new questions. Historically, doctrine has developed as the church grows in understanding the realities and words which have been handed down in Scripture and tradition. Frequently, this growing understanding comes from the experience of the people of God or some conflict with standard norms. We are living in such a moment. Where is the Holy Spirit leading the church? How can the core of the rich tradition be preserved at the same time as it is expanded to address this new reality?

What follows is but one thread in a mighty large tapestry that needs to be woven. I am going to apply one of Cardinal Dulles's principles to one text of Genesis. There are certainly other principles of doctrinal development that can be applied. There are a multitude of other biblical texts that need to be brought into play. This is but one example of how we can start to think about this subject, not an overall program for development of teaching on gendered identity or sexual morality.

APPLYING THE FIFTH PRINCIPLE

Dulles's fifth principle states that "no church teaching of the past directly solves a question that was not asked at the time."[5] Correlatively, "whenever the state of the evidence about a question materially changes, we have a new question which cannot be answered by appealing to old authorities."[6] How might this work when dealing with church teaching on LGBTQ persons?

The judgment that homosexual genital activity is disordered is based, in good part, on an appeal to the Genesis narrative where, on the sixth day, God created human beings "male and female" and gave them the mandate to "be fruitful and multiply" (Gen 1:27–28). From this text, church teaching deduces a strong gender binary where persons are either male, with masculine characteristics, or female, with feminine characteristics, the two being complementary.

Marriage brings the two into relationship to be fruitful, so that every sexual act must be open to the conception of a child. In this framework, the sexual identity and activity of LGBTQ persons falls outside the norm. Let us consider this line of thinking.

According to biblical scholarship, Genesis 1 is not a historical record of an event. In terms of literary genre, it is a myth of origins. It is a religious narrative constructed in a six-day sequence to teach that God created everything that exists—day and night, sky and water, dry land and plants,

5. Dulles, *The Survival of Dogma*, 179.
6. Dulles, *The Survival of Dogma*, 180.

sun and moon, fish and birds, all kinds of animals that creep and walk on the earth, and all people. After the initial act of creation, to provide for continuation, God blessed all living creatures with the gift of fertility. And God saw that it was good, and then rested.

For centuries, church teaching interpreted the six-day timeline of this narrative literally, but it no longer does so. In our day, the state of the evidence on the question has materially changed. Scientific knowledge of the age of the universe and the long history of the evolution of life on earth has cast the six days back into their proper literary form.

Far from insisting on a literal understanding of creation in six days, church teaching has developed a sophisticated reading that honors the religious intent of the story while also respecting modern scientific knowledge. The point is that God created everything, not how.

Embedded in this narrative of origin, the description of human beings who are created male and female in the image of God is meant generically to include all human beings. It writes humans as a category of creature into the creation story as part of the whole wondrous scenario, with an additional responsibility to care for the rest.

To put it plainly, Genesis 1 is not dealing with issues of sexual orientation. Just as Paul's writing about Adam's sin was not intended to teach about the origin of humanity in a single couple, so too the description of human beings created male and female in Genesis 1 was not intended to define God's will for a gender binary. Rather, the text intends to bring all people into view as God's good creatures and responsible members of the community of creation.

Using Genesis 1 today as a source that teaches that heterosexual orientation is the only God-approved way to be human does not work because this text is not dealing with the question of LGBTQ persons. Coming to the text with a prior conviction about a gender binary, church authorities read it into the text. But biblical scholarship today shows that the text does not teach this.

As with the six days, so too with the two genders. The words about male and female and the mandate to be fruitful are embedded in the larger creation story and share its literary genre. They need not be interpreted literally. A small door opens, one of many that are possible, where the development of doctrine becomes thinkable.

WISDOM ON DIVINE LOVE

Searching the Scriptures for a way to think about LGBTQ persons in a framework different from Genesis, we might well begin with a creation text from the Book of Wisdom. It makes a radical claim about God who creates: "For thou lovest all things that exist, and hast loathing for none of the things which thou hast made, for thou wouldst not have made anything if thou hadst hated it" (Wis 11:24).

What exquisite reasoning! From the vast spiraling galaxies to the tiniest nematodes, an outpouring of divine love makes and sustains all beings. Without that love, there would be nothing at all—nothing.

Of course, this includes LGBTQ persons. They are beloved creatures, called and gifted in their body and sexuality, their spirit, mind, and heart, their power and agency, strengths and limitations. Their very existence outside the norm of heterosexuality bears witness to the truth that God is the creative source of the whole sexuality and gender spectrum, "for thou wouldst not have made anything if thou hadst hated it."

The great holy mystery whom people call *God* has a heart for all creatures. When sin and suffering mar the lives of LGBTQ persons, the same ineffable Love who makes all beings that exist also moves with compassion to heal, forgive, redeem, and liberate. In a psalmist's beautiful words, God "heals the brokenhearted and binds up their wounds. [God] determines the number of the stars; [and] gives to all of them their names" (Ps 147:3–4).

As with every beloved creature, the faithful love of God seeks to save and bring them to fulfillment through thick and thin. Violence against LGBTQ persons is on the upswing. Statistics show that LGBTQ persons, especially teens, experience mental health struggles and suicidality at much higher rates than the general heterosexual population. So much the more is the life-giving care of God with those who struggle in this way, willing their full flourishing.

Such mercy is not a sideline or a minor theme in Scripture, but its major revelation. Jesus who is Emmanuel, "God with us," embodied this love in his ministry, especially in his interactions with marginalized people, as so much biblical scholarship about LGBTQ persons rightly emphasizes.

This is but one avenue along which our thinking could proceed in creative fidelity to Scripture and tradition. For over two thousand years, church teaching has been a living tradition that develops. "For as the centuries succeed one another, the church constantly moves forward toward the fullness of divine truth until the words of God reach their complete fulfillment" (*DV* 8). The church is ever on the way, fleshing out more fully the meaning of the gospel in cultural contexts that emerge over time.

The impetus to new understandings or the reform of older ideas comes from a variety of sources, including the lived experience of believers, crises and conflicts demanding new gospel answers, prayer, meditation on Scripture, new theological analyses, the insights of secular learning, the evolution of human institutions, and the examples and instruction given by persons of goodwill. In our day, the voices, struggles, and graced witness of LGBTQ persons and those who love and support them are an irreplaceable resource in this process. "By their fruits you will know them" (Matt 7:16 NABRE).

3

HOW TO READ THE BIBLE'S "CLOBBER PASSAGES" ON HOMOSEXUALITY

Amy-Jill Levine, PhD

In 2017, I wrote an article for the Australian Broadcasting Company titled "Not Good to Be Alone: Rethinking the Bible and Homosexuality." The prompt for this piece was the debate in Australia over same-sex marriage. I sought to list alternative readings for the so-called clobber passages[1]—Genesis 1—2; 19:1–38; Leviticus 18:22; 20:13; Romans 1:25–27; 1 Corinthians 6:9–11; 1 Timothy 1:9–10; and Jude 6–7—deployed to exclude and condemn queer people.

Some conservative interpreters presume the texts self-

1. The term "clobber passages" likely derives from Letha Scanzoni and Virginia Ramey Mollenkott, *Is the Homosexual My Neighbor? A Positive Christian Response* (Harper & Row, 1978) in discussion of how clergy "clobbered them" with specific passages (with thanks to Alexander Geller for this research).

evidently reject consensual same-sex relations. However, not only are the meanings of some texts obscure, but interpreting those texts with limited, literalist lenses is, theologically speaking, to suggest that G-d has nothing else to say and to put the Holy Spirit out of business.

Some liberal interpreters insist that Jesus abrogated Levitical laws and that Paul's rejection of same-sex relations comes from his "rabbinic background." The first point, concerning Jesus, is wrong: Jesus comes not to abolish Torah but to fulfill it (Matt 5:17; "fulfill" connotes elucidating a fuller meaning to the commandments, not nullifying or abandoning them; see Mark 7:7–8). The second point, concerning Paul, is both anachronistic and inaccurate. Rabbinic sources substantially postdate Paul, and they offer several different views about sexuality and gender. The end (full inclusion for LGBTQ Christians) does not justify the means (throwing the Old Testament and Jewish tradition under the bus).

We can do better.

My original essay began with the biblical texts; this chapter begins with guidelines for biblical interpretation.

THE IMPORTANCE OF INTERPRETATION

Biblical verses can support opposing views: slavery versus abolition; women's equality versus keeping women subordinate or in a complementarian (separate but equal) role; pro-life versus pro-choice; environmental mastery versus environmental preservation; and so on. Therefore, speaking of "misuse" of the Bible is often the wrong approach. People with whom we disagree do not think they are misusing or misreading. But, as the adage goes, the Bible should be a rock on which one stands, not a rock thrown to damage.

For biblical interpretation regarding queer concerns, six guidelines are helpful.

First, we should treat the Bible less as an ethical answer book and more as a book prompting the right questions. That is why, for example, Genesis 34, a story about a seduction or a rape, ends not with resolution but with a question. It does teach, however, that rape must be addressed, that rape impacts the families of both the perpetrator and the victim, and that responding to violence with more violence doesn't work.

Second, "the Bible, gender, and sexuality" is not just an academic concern: it impacts lives. Therefore, before making pronouncements about the topic, it is helpful to speak with people who identify as queer and their families, friends, and allies, as well as with those who hold to more traditionalist approaches. To speak about a group is usually more successful when one speaks first to people within that group.

Third, demonizing people is wrong, for they too are in the divine image. Therefore, we should listen to people with whom we disagree. The point is not to subject ourselves to more clobbering; it is to see why and how the people who disagree with our views read the way they do. For example, people who would restrict women from serving in ecclesial leadership positions are following 1 Corinthians 14:33–36 and 1 Timothy 2:11–15. Their restriction is usually based not in misogyny but in a high view of biblical authority. Alternatively, people who support women's leadership may cite Miriam the prophet (Exod 15:20), Deborah the judge (Judg 4—5), Esther the queen, Phoebe the deacon (Rom 16:1), Junia the apostle (Rom 16:7), and so on. They too may have a high view of biblical authority. Conversation rather than condemnation or cancelling is in order.

Fourth, the Bible is less a one-size-fits-all guide and more an anthology produced in different contexts, featuring different voices and addressing different needs. Nor should we attempt to live exactly as the Bible advocates, since that would make us, for example, first-century Corinthians. Those historical contexts also matter, since the Bible's authors, no matter how "inspired," cannot escape their own social setting.

Fifth, the clobber passages are not the only source of teaching. The Bible engages in internal conversation, and one verse can be interpreted in consideration of another. For example, Jesus compares weightier commandments, doing justice and mercy, and less weighty ones, like tithing mint (see Matt 23:23). He names, as did fellow Jews, the greatest commandments to be love of G-d (see Matt 22:38–39 and Mark 12:30–33, citing Deut 6:5) and love of neighbor (citing Lev 19:18). These commandments should guide interpretation of the others.

For interpretation, we also have tradition (how the text has been interpreted differently over time), science, history, insights from people from multiple social locations, and revelation (the work of the Holy Spirit, which may be how most people eventually concluded that slavery is sinful, despite the Bible's endorsement).

Finally, there is bibliolatry—worshiping the Bible, turning it into an idol—rather than worshiping the deity to whom the Bible points. Instead of saying "the Bible says it; I believe it," sometimes we are more faithful by saying, "the Bible says it; let's discuss."[2] We need to determine *what* the text says, given both that it was originally written in Hebrew or Greek and that translation is more an art than a science. We also need to determine *why* it says what it says. Does the injunction apply to all times and places, or is it for a particular group

2. See examples in Amy-Jill Levine, *Jesus for Everyone, Not Just Christians* (HarperOne, 2024).

at a particular place and time? In many cases, our conclusions may well appear "indistinctly, as in a mirror" (1 Corinthians 13:12).

GENESIS 1—2

Genesis 1:27 says, "God created humankind [Hebrew *adam*; the NABRE reads "mankind"] in the image of God… male and female" (author's translation). Our first point: male and female humans are created equally; everyone is in the image and likeness of the divine.

Second, Hebrew, Aramaic, and Greek are gendered languages—Hebrew and Aramaic have masculine and feminine, and Greek has masculine, feminine, and neuter. In the Bible, masculine verbs and adjectives describe G-d. But for G-d there can be no "sex assigned at birth." In terms of gender, the Bible describes G-d as both masculine warrior (e.g., Exod 15:3; Isa 42:13) and birthing, loving mother (e.g., Deut 32:18; Isa 66:13); so this G-d, whose lower body is not seen, transcends gender and sexual categories.

Third, from Genesis 1:27 comes the view that people must be either male or female. Alternatively, we can look at the verse as a merism: using two contrasting words to suggest a whole. Part of Genesis 1—2 concerns division: separating water from dry land, day from night, the workweek and the Sabbath. But part is about G-d's all-encompassing nature. To say G-d created the heavens and the earth also means that G-d created everything in between. To say that G-d created night and day also means that G-d created dawn and twilight. Thus, G-d created male and female and everyone in between.

For Paul, "There is no longer male and female; for all of you are one in Christ Jesus" (Gal 3:28). Gender roles do not matter in relation to the divine. And Paul's fellow Jews would agree.

The Talmud, a compendium of Jewish thought, recognizes several gendered bodies: not only male and female but also *androgynos* (having male and female characteristics or "intersex"), *tumtum* (whose genitals are not clearly male or female), *aylonit* (identified female at birth but lacks female characteristics associated with puberty), *saris* (identified male at birth but lacking male characteristics associated with puberty), *saris chama* (a male born sterile, e.g., lacking testicles), and the *saris adam* (a castrated male).[3] While Deuteronomy 23:1 bars men with crushed testicles or lacking a penis (i.e., eunuchs) from admission to the assembly, Isaiah 56:4–5 affirms eunuchs who keep the Sabbath. Rabbinic Judaism recognizes them as community members: the Mishna, *m. Yevamot* 8.6, for example, begins, "A priest, a eunuch by nature, who married an Israelite girl, feeds her heave offering." Ancient Jews, including Jesus, were not literalists. They knew their Scripture needed to be interpreted, and they knew that gender and sexuality were complex subjects. And of course, some Jews will insist that there are only "male" and "female" and that any other identification is an aberration.

Fourth, G-d commands the humans to "be fruitful and multiply" (Gen 1:28). Some interpreters argue that this first commandment both limits sexual intercourse to fertile heterosexual couples and disallows birth control. The argument

3. The definitions all require nuance. For a brief summary, see Rachel Scheinerman, "The Eight Genders in the Talmud," My Jewish Learning (https://www.myjewishlearning.com/article/the-eight-genders-in-the-talmud/). For a detailed study, see Max K. Strassfeld, *Trans Talmud: Androgynes and Eunuchs in Rabbinic Literature* (University of California Press, 2023) and Strassfeld's summary, "Transing the Talmud or Reading the Talmud 'Badly,'" *Ancient Jew Review* (September 28, 2023), https://www.ancientjewreview.com/read/2023/9/28/transing-the-talmud-or-reading-the-talmud-badly.

fails on multiple levels. The text is an endorsement of procreation (and so sexual relations), not a limitation of sexual acts. It is an entirely positive "thou shalt" rather than a negative "thou shalt not." Such restrictive readings also prohibit sexual intercourse between (heteronormative) couples who cannot reproduce, which denies the goodness of creation and the value of intimate contact between couples who love each other. We might also conclude that this first commandment was completed in Genesis 11:8–9, when humanity, following the fall of the tower of Babel, filled the earth.

Fifth, following Genesis 1:1–2:4 comes a second creation story, Genesis 2:4–25, the one in which G-d creates a woman from the human being's (Hebrew *ha'adam*; NABRE: "man's") side (NABRE: "rib"). From this narrative comes the refrain: "God created Adam and Eve, not Adam and Steve." G-d created Steve too. While some claim that G-d created women as the man's "helper" (Gen 2:18, 20) because only women (and not, for example, sheep or ostriches) can help men reproduce, this notion reduces women to wombs, strips value from women who for whatever reason (for example, infertility, menopause, the gift of celibacy, and so on) cannot or do not reproduce, and excludes childless couples. The "helper" (Hebrew *ezer*, a term predicated also of G-d) is the one who mirrors to the solitary human being what it means to be human.

Marriage and children can be terrific (I speak from personal experience), but they are not the only markers of life abundant. Jesus never married and never had children. Paul states in 1 Corinthians 7:8 that it is better to remain unmarried, as he is, and that the Corinthians would do well to imitate him. Revelation 14:4 praises 144,000 male virgins "who have not known a woman." The biblical text is in dialogue, with places for both heterosexual marriages and for other domestic arrangements.

GENESIS 19

Genesis 19, the story of Sodom and Gomorrah, has nothing to do with consensual sexual relations; Sodom's sins range from inhospitality to attempted rape. Ezekiel 16:49 reads, "This was the guilt of your sister Sodom; she...did not aid the poor and needy." Sirach 16:8 states that G-d condemned the people because of their arrogance.

The men of Sodom (the Hebrew *anshe*, the masculine plural term, can include women—which broadens their concern beyond male-male relations) seek to "know" (Gen 19:5), that is, have sexual relations with, the two strangers to whom Abraham's nephew Lot offered hospitality (who turn out to be angels). Attempting to protect his guests, Lot offers the mob his two virgin daughters—another horrific subject that receives no attention in the rush to condemn "sodomites." The angels rescue Lot and his household, and G-d destroys the city.

The scene replays in Judges 19. A Levite and his concubine (another sexual role) seek shelter in the Benjaminite city of Gibeah. A man from the tribe of Ephraim—like Lot, a foreigner in the city—invites them home. When the locals seek to "know" the Levite, the host offers them his virgin daughter and the Levite's concubine: "Ravish them and do whatever you want to them; but against this man do not do such a vile thing" (Judg 19:24). In the biblical mentality, and for many today, rape of women is seen as less heinous than rape of men. The male guest, or perhaps the host, then tosses out the concubine, whom the Benjaminites "raped...and abused... all through the night" (Judg 19:25). Again, the account is not about consent, let alone love. Like the story of Dinah in Genesis 34, Judges 19 shows that violence only leads to more violence, even as it forces the reader to confront the real sins

Judges 19 and then Judges 20 depict: domestic abuse, rape, kidnapping, sex trafficking, and murder.

LEVITICUS 18:22; 20:13

Leviticus 18:22 in Hebrew literally says, "and with a male [Hebrew *zakhar*] not will you lie the lyings of a woman [*mishkave isha*]; it is an abomination." Leviticus 20:13 adds the penalty of capital punishment. No ancient Jewish text shows these laws enacted.

The meaning of "lyings of a woman" remains debated. The expression only appears in these two verses. If the text read, "Don't put your penis there," we'd have a more pointed interpretation. To conclude that "lyings of a woman" is an idiom for male anal intercourse is a good speculation, but we cannot know for certain.

Our next question concerns the law's purpose. Here are the top five answers.

A first claim is that the text forbids Israelite men from engaging in sexual relations with other men, because that's what Canaanites did. There is no evidence that Canaanites celebrated such relationships. Canaanites also engaged in heterosexual intercourse.

A second is that the injunction intends to prevent male rape in war. Again, nothing suggests such a limitation.

Another claim is that Leviticus forbids homosexual relations because two men cannot procreate. Probably not. The Bible never forbids men having relations with pregnant or postmenopausal women. (Sarah conceives in her nineties, but that's a one-off.) Nor are sterile men prohibited from sexual relations. Nor does the Old Testament forbid masturbation. (In Genesis 38:9, Onan—from whom we get the term *onanism*—engages not in masturbation but in a form of birth control by "spilling his seed on the ground.")

A fourth claim extends the third: homosexual relations are forbidden because they decrease the birth rate. The point is silly. Gay and bisexual men can and do father children.

Fifth is the claim that anal intercourse (if that is what the commandment prohibits) leads to anal tearing; therefore, Leviticus promotes male health. Again, doubtful: the text does not forbid heterosexual anal intercourse.

What is the purpose of these verses? Here's my take: they concern category maintenance designed to organize life and avoid chaos. To be holy is to be separate, so practices are needed to separate the holy from the profane. Genesis opens with such maintenance: separating light and day, waters above from waters below, Sabbath and other days. Leviticus continues the process: Leviticus 19:19 forbids crossbreeding animals, planting a field with two kinds of seed, and wearing a garment made from two different materials; Leviticus 20:26 separates Israel from other nations.

Leviticus assigns gender roles as its authors understood them: men do what the authors considered appropriate for men, and the same for women. For a male to "lie with a male the lyings of a woman" puts the second man into the woman's role, which creates category confusion. The injunctions probably concern male-male anal intercourse, because such intercourse contravenes the idea that men do the penetrating and women are the penetrated.

If Leviticus prohibits male-male anal intercourse, now what? Seven points to consider:

First, Leviticus says nothing about lesbians. For Leviticus: no penis, no semen ejaculated, no problem. Thus, Leviticus has a different definition of sexuality than we do today.

Second, Leviticus primarily concerns life in the land of Israel. This injunction does no good for gay friends in Tel

Aviv, but it may be irrelevant for those cohabiting in Nashville.

Third, Leviticus addresses the people of Israel, not Gentiles. Since most Christians today are Gentiles (i.e., non-Jews), laws given to Israel, unless the New Testament repeats them, are irrelevant. Christians need no more attend to Leviticus 18 and 20 than they need attend to Leviticus 11:10, which prohibits eating shellfish.

Fourth, the injunctions occur in the context of familial relations. Leviticus 18:9, for example, forbids brother-sister relations. The only other time the Hebrew *mishkave*, "lyings of," appears in Torah also concerns incest. Genesis 49:4 describes Reuben as engaged "the lyings of your father": that is, Reuben had relations with Jacob's wife, Bilhah. Thus, Leviticus 18:22 may primarily concern incestuous relations (males in the same family).

Fifth, if the commandment does forbid male-male anal intercourse—which seems to me likely—it need not be read as forbidding other forms of male-male sexual expression.

Sixth, if the text is about categories, it could be understood as saying: you, male person, shall not lie with a male as with a woman—that is, gay relationships need not correspond to a "husband and wife" model. Did the author of Leviticus intend this reading? Not likely. But the text can support it.

Finally, a page from Jesus's playbook: Jesus cites Genesis 2:24, the uniting of the first man and woman by G-d, to condemn divorce, even though Deuteronomy 22 permits divorce. Reading Deuteronomy in light of Genesis, Jesus determines that Genesis is the more important. We can similarly read Leviticus in light of Genesis. In Genesis 2:18, G-d states, "It is not good for the human being (*ha'adam*) to be alone. I will make him a helper as his partner." If it is not good for a human being to be alone, queer people should not be prevented from finding their "helpers" who mirror back to them their own humanity and complete them.

JESUS

Jesus says nothing about "homosexuality" (the word was not coined until the nineteenth century). But he has much to say about sexual relations and gender roles. For example, he splits up families: "Whoever comes to me and does not hate father and mother, wife and children, brothers and sisters, yes, and even life itself, cannot be my disciple" (Luke 14:26). He commends celibacy: "Those who belong to this age marry and are given in marriage; but those who are considered worthy of a place in that age and in the resurrection from the dead neither marry nor are given in marriage" (Luke 20:34–35). He notices "eunuchs who have been so from birth, and...eunuchs who have been made eunuchs by others," and he praises "eunuchs who have made themselves eunuchs for the sake of the kingdom of heaven" (Matt 19:12; see also Acts 8:26–39). Jesus even warns against pregnancy and lactation (see Matt 24:19; Mark 13:17; Luke 21:23). On the other hand, he also provides wine for a wedding (John 2:1–11). (I do wonder if John placed the first sign at the wedding of Cana in order to assure fellow followers that Jesus endorsed marriage along with celibacy.)

Dangers of Citing Jesus

Seeking to enfranchise queer Christians, some theologians set up Judaism as the negative foil. They are not (as far as I know) antisemites; they are rather following a long tradition of biblical scholarship that depicts first-century Judaism as toxic in order to distinguish Jesus from his own people.

For example, it's common to view purity laws as particularly oppressive to queer people, so that Jesus, by abrogating purity laws, enfranchises the marginalized. The argument not only fails, but it also introduces or reinforces antisemitism. One need not make Judaism look bad in order to make Jesus look good.

When Jesus touches a corpse or a man suffering from a skin disease, or when he allows a woman suffering vaginal or uterine bleeding to touch him, he is not abrogating purity laws. To the contrary, he restores these individuals to ritual purity. Nor does any law forbid touching ritually impure people (and most people are impure most of the time). Corpses are impure, but burying them is a mitzvah, a commandment. Women who menstruate or who have just given birth are impure, but they are not removed from society. Neither are men who ejaculate.

A related, and similarly incorrect view, sees Jesus as participating in a Torah-light system over and against what is described as Pharisaic rigorism and legalism. Wrong again, since Jesus makes the Torah stricter: to the commandment against murder, he forbids anger (Matt 5:22); to the commandment against adultery, he forbids thinking about it (Matt 5:28). While he promotes justice over tithing, he insists that tithing be done as well (Matt 23:23).

Sometimes Jesus is seen as welcoming queer people because he welcomes "sinners and tax collectors." Here is more category confusion. Sinners and tax collectors were not people who ate bacon, slept with menstruating women, or touched men who had just ejaculated. The issue is not purity. The people Jesus meets at table are the equivalents of traitors, sex traffickers, loan sharks, and drug pushers. They were not "outcast": they appear in synagogues and the temple; their multiple friends attend their banquets. The issue is not welcoming the marginal or the outcast. Rather, Jesus is calling sinners, those who deliberately harm others, to repent. I see no reason to put queer people in the "sinner" category or to call them to repent from being who they are.

ROMANS 1:26–27

Paul explains to the Roman assembly how Gentiles failed to recognize the one G-d in the wonders of creation or the promptings of their own conscience. Instead, they "worshiped and served the creature rather than the Creator" (Rom 1:25). Therefore, Paul states, G-d handed them over to "dishonorable passions [Greek: *pathe atimias*]" so that "their females quit natural use [*physiken chresin*] for [use] beside [i.e., contrary to] nature [*para physin*], and likewise even the males, giving up natural use of females, burned with passion for each other, males with males working shameless acts" (Rom 1:26–27, author's translation).

Our first problem is defining "natural use." While some interpreters claim that "*natural* use" means that a penis fits better into a vagina than into other apertures, the claim ignores the lack of injunctions against not only heterosexual anal intercourse but also oral sex, intercrural sex (a typical form of pederasty), and other forms of sexual expression. Regarding women's "unnatural" activity, Augustine and Clement of Alexandria thought Paul was talking about intercourse that did not lead to procreation, such as heterosexual anal intercourse. John Chrysostom reads lesbian activity. Church proclamations have not been consistent over time (as we see today, for example, regarding the question of women deacons).

Our second problem is that what Paul sees as "nature" is rather an argument from culture. Elsewhere Paul asks, "Does not nature itself teach you that if a man wears long hair, it is degrading to him, but if a woman has long hair, it is her glory?" (1 Cor 11:14–15). No, nature does not teach that long hair on males is degrading, as lions, peacocks, and Warner Sallman's 1940 painting *Head of Christ* all show. Nor are same-sex relations absent from the natural world, as sheep, lions, and female bottlenose dolphins demonstrate.

Some commentators argue that Paul addresses heterosexual men who turned from what is "natural" for them, meaning heterosexual intercourse, to what is "contrary to nature" for them, meaning intercourse with men. Others think that Romans 1 concerns orgies, given that the immediate narrative context speaks about lust, dishonorable passions, and shameless acts. While I find neither claim compelling, these speculations demonstrate that Paul's language is not clear.

Next, Paul uses the expression "contrary to nature" (Rom 11:24) to describe how Gentiles were "cut from what is by nature [*kata physin*] a wild olive tree and grafted, contrary to nature [*para physin*], into a cultivated olive tree." An act contrary to nature creates being in a right relationship with G-d.

Finally, while Romans 1:32 condemns Gentiles who "know God's decree, that those who practice such things deserve to die" since "they not only do them but even applaud others who practice them," the next verses (2:1–3) condemn anyone who judges: "Therefore you have no excuse, whoever you are, when you judge others; for in passing judgment on another you condemn yourself, because you, the judge, are doing the very same things" (Rom 2:1). Such a condemnation should give us pause when we judge others regarding matters of gender and sexuality.

1 CORINTHIANS 6:9–11

In his first (extant) Letter to the Corinthians, Paul says, "Do you not know that wrongdoers will not inherit the kingdom of G-d? Do not be deceived! *pornoi*, idolaters, adulterers, *malakoi*, *arsenokotai*, thieves, the greedy, drunkards, revilers, robbers—none of these will inherit the kingdom of God" (1 Cor 6:9–10, author's translation). Defining the key Greek terms is our first problem. The second is determining why Paul included these elements in his vice list.

Pornoi, whence "pornography," concerns improper sexual behavior. English translations range from "fornicator" to "sexually immoral" to the quaint "whoremongers." But as we saw with the Old Testament's lack of explicit reference to lesbians, definitions of what is sexually improper change over time. *Pornoi* could be sex workers and/or their clients, or people who have sexual intercourse outside of marriage. *Porneia*—illegal sexual behavior—receives different definitions over time and place.

For *malakoi*, translations include "male prostitutes," "effeminate," "catamite" (a prepubescent boy kept for pederastic relations), "homosexuals," "sexual perverts," and "those who make women of themselves." *Malakos*, meaning "soft," connotes passive sexual activity as opposed to active and suggests indolence rather than discipline—a couch potato rather than a jogger.

Arsenokoitai is a neologism from *arsen*, "male" and *koite* (whence "coitus"), derived from Greek for "bed." Although translated as "perverts" or "sodomites," *arsenokoitai* could also refer to pimps or procurers. Martin Luther thought it referred to *Knabenschanders*, "boy molesters" or what we would call "pedophiles."

What these words meant for Paul and his Corinthian audience we can only guess. It's possible Paul coined *arsenokoitai* based on the Greek translation of Leviticus 20:13, which in forbidding "lyings of a woman" reads *arsenos koitan gynaikos* (of a male, bed/sexual intercourse/of a woman). While some suggest that *malakoi* connotes "bottoms" and *arsenokotai* connotes "tops," there is no reason for Paul to have created a neologism.

Paul notes that the vices represent what his audience used to practice, prior to baptism (1 Cor 6:11). The assembly members, now "washed" and "sanctified," are no longer greedy, drunkards, revilers, and robbers. But the baptized queer person is still queer. Greed, alcoholism, narcissism, stealing—all these harm community and self. Harm comes not from queer identity, but from those who condemn queer individuals, especially queer youth, for being who they are.

1 TIMOTHY 1:10

This epistle, written in Paul's name, offers another vice list. Again, we have *pornoi* and *arsenokoitai*, now along with *andrapodistes*, "slave-dealers" or "kidnappers." The terms together may suggest coerced, commercial transactions: the "fornicator" who procures an enslaved person for sexual purposes, the pimp or brothelkeeper, and the enslaver. For the enslaved, consent is irrelevant.

JUDE 6–7

According to the enigmatic Genesis 6:1–4, "sons of God" had sexual relations with "daughters of men." Drawing from the pre-Christian Jewish text *1 Enoch* or associated traditions, Jude 6 explains that G-d imprisoned these "fallen" angels to await judgment day. Now comes Jude's clobber verse, alluding to Genesis 19: "Like Sodom and Gomorrah and the cities around them, which with the same customs, acted in a sexually immoral way (Greek: *ek-porneusomai*, from *porneia*) and went away after other flesh (Greek: *sarkos heteras*)" (Jude 6–7, author's translation). Genesis 19 concerns an attempted rape of strangers, who are, in fact, angels. Jude reverses the motif in mentioning angels who have sexual relations with women. For Jude, the issue is divine-human coupling, which is contrary to angelic nature, since, as Jesus puts it, angels neither marry nor are given in marriage (see Matt 22:30; Mark 12:25; Luke 20:35). The text has nothing to do with homosexuality—nor is angelic copulation (to date) a political or ecclesial issue.

OTHER PASSAGES

The Bible insists that the body is "in the image and likeness of God" (Gen 1:26) and "a temple of the Holy Spirit" (1 Cor 6:19). Psalm 139:14 proclaims, "I praise you, for I am fearfully and wonderfully made." The Bible celebrates sexual desire: "Let him kiss me with the kisses of his mouth! For your love is better than wine" (Song 1:2); "May her breasts always satisfy you; may you be intoxicated always by her love" (Prov 5:19). It acknowledges geriatric sexuality. When Sarah learns that she will have a child, she "laughed to herself, saying, 'After I have grown old, and my husband is old, shall I have [sexual] pleasure [Hebrew *edna*, "pleasure," a cognate of *Eden*]?" (Gen 18:12). She will. Good for her.

Ruth and Naomi model a family comprised of two women. Genesis 2:24 explains that a man leaves his father and mother and clings (Hebrew *davak*) to his wife, and they become one flesh. "One flesh" does not mean permanent sexual intercourse (which would be awkward): it means to become a new family. Ruth 1:14 states that Ruth clung (*davak*) to Naomi. Despite the note in Genesis 2:24 regarding what the husband is to do, in the Bible, it is generally the woman who leaves her parents and joins the man.

David eulogizes Jonathan, "Greatly beloved were you to me; your love to me was wonderful, surpassing the love of women" (2 Sam 1:26). David, who had multiple wives, including Jonathan's sister Michal, could be making a politically opportune speech, could have loved Jonathan like a brother, or could have loved Jonathan....

Paul uses "gender-bending" language when he speaks of "being in the pain of childbirth" (Gal 4:19). According to John, when a soldier pierces Jesus's side with a spear, "at once blood and water came out" (John 19:34). The image suggests parturition, whereby Jesus gives birth to the church. Julian of Norwich writes, "The human mother can tenderly lay the child on her breast, but our tender Mother Jesus can lead us directly into his own tender breast through his sweet broken-open side."[4]

All readers can use the hermeneutics of imagination to find ourselves in the biblical text. There are no Japanese, Kenyan, or Chilean people in the Bible, but Japanese, Kenyans, and Chileans can and do relate to biblical characters. There have been queer people throughout history, although for the most part they go unremarked. They are likely populating the text, from Genesis to Revelation. We can imagine them to be there.

FINAL THOUGHTS

Biblical texts require interpretation. Lives depend on our interpretations. Queer people should be and can be affirmed

4. *Julian of Norwich: Showings*, trans. Edmund Colledge, OSA, and James Walsh, SJ, Classics of Western Spirituality (Paulist Press, 1977), 298.

by gracious readings of the Bible. The clobber passages, if they do not meet the criteria of love, can be stripped of their power. And if we cannot find affirmation of our personal identity, our ability to love G-d and others is stunted.

As the great RuPaul asks, "If you can't love yourself, how the hell you gonna love someone else....Can I get an amen?"

4

THE BIBLE DOES NOT CONDEMN LGBTQ PEOPLE

The Rev. Brandan Robertson

As a Christian pastor and theologian who also is openly gay, I am asked almost daily how I can justify my "lifestyle" as an LGBTQ person with my Christian faith. For years this question perplexed me and caused me to stay in the closet, believing that God desired for me do my best either to become heterosexual or to repress this "sinful" desire within me to align with what I believed was the "clear teaching of Scripture" regarding LGBTQ identity and relationships.

My chief concern has always been to honor God and to live in alignment with the truth revealed in Scripture. And so for the past decade, I have devoted my life to studying and teaching what the Bible says not just about homosexuality, but about sexuality and gender in general. My studies have taken me across the country and around the world, visiting ancient biblical sites, consulting with the world's leading biblical scholars and theologians, obtaining two degrees in biblical theology, and leading me to a doctorate program focused on sexuality and gender in Scripture.

I guess you could say that I wanted to make sure that I was right on this one; and as a Protestant, one of the chief ways to have confidence in the correctness of one's beliefs about any issue is through a robust study of the Bible.

After ten years of critical study, I have become utterly convinced that the Bible does not condemn LGBTQ identities or consensual sexual expression and relationships. But rather than offering a robust, detailed examination of each of the "clobber passages" of the Bible (Scripture verses cited as condemnation of LGBTQ people), I want to offer a summary of the explanation I give when asked what the Bible teaches about LGBTQ identity.

I do this in hopes that it might help other LGBTQ Christians and allies when they are confronted by those who remain convinced that LGBTQ identity and relationships are sinful.

Essentially, the six references to homosexual sex in Scripture are *all* references not to consensual, loving, same-sex behavior, but references to sexual exploitation, abuse, and idolatry. If you open the Bible to any of the clobber passages and read the entire chapter to which each singular verse or story belongs, you will find multiple references to the worship of idols and to other heinous, exploitative, and abusive sins.

For example, in Leviticus 18:22, "You shall not lie with a male as with a woman; it is an abomination" (v. 22), one only needs to return to the beginning of the chapter to gain an understanding of the *context* of this condemnation:

> The LORD spoke to Moses, saying: "Speak to the Israelites and say to them: I am the LORD your God.

> You shall not do as they do in the land of Egypt, where you lived, and you shall not do as they do in the land of Canaan, to which I am bringing you. You shall not follow their statutes. (Lev 18:1–3)

The context of the chapter is God giving the Israelites a series of commands to not engage in the practices and customs of surrounding pagan nations. Notice, as New Testament scholar Amy-Jill Levine noted in the previous chapter, that this list of commands is aimed only at the Israelites within the land of Israel and no one else. These aren't universal moral laws, but laws specific to the religious context of the ancient Israelite people. This *doesn't* mean that *none* of the behaviors condemned in Leviticus should not be condemned by modern Christians—of course, many of them should. But the particular context of the Book of Leviticus itself is to dictate the conduct of the Israelites in the land of Israel, keeping them ritually and culturally distinct from the practices of the pagan nations they found themselves in the midst of.

For instance, the pagan nations of Egypt and Canaan were not devoted to the one true God of the Jewish people, but to a pantheon of gods and goddesses who required various practices and sacrificial offerings that would have been considered blasphemous to Jewish people. These cultures also permitted their male citizens to sexually exploit *anyone* of a lower social status as a display of domination and superiority, and very little evidence exists of widespread affirmation of romantic relationships between people of the same sex. Because Leviticus 18 specifically names the practices of the Egyptians and Canaanites, every following command in Leviticus 18, then, should be read considering this narrow and specific context.

In both Leviticus 18 and Leviticus 20:13 (the other reference to same-sex sex in Leviticus) the context is the impure behaviors of these specific pagan nations. For instance, some ancient Egyptians worshiped the goddess Sakhnet, and every year they would host a feast in her honor that involved drunkenness, dancing, and ritual sex. Often, the sex that would occur in these rituals was between people of the same sex.

There is some evidence that the ancient Canaanites also engaged in such ritual prostitution to worship their goddesses Astarte and Ishtar, among others, though admittedly the evidence for ritual sexual practices is scant. Similarly, almost every other sexual prohibition in Leviticus 18 refers to an incestuous practice rather than other general sexual behavior, which could also suggest that the author of Leviticus had incestuous same-sex behavior in mind with this prohibition.

Considering this context, *whatever* Leviticus 18:22 and Leviticus 20:13 are condemning must be related to either (or both) the idolatrous ritual practices of the Egyptians and Canaanites, or to same-sex *abusive* or *incestuous* relationships between males that was common in these cultures. This does not include loving and consensual same-sex relationships, which we have very little evidence were widely permitted in either of these cultures.

The same argument also applies when examining the most famous New Testament "condemnation" of homosexuality in Romans 1. The entire chapter is a description of how Roman culture descended into idolatry and then into grave immorality. They go from knowing God (v. 21), to worshiping created things (v. 23). Then, in the context of that idolatry, we're told:

> Therefore God gave them up in the lusts of their hearts to impurity, to the degrading of their bodies among themselves, because they exchanged the truth about God for a lie and worshiped and served

> the creature rather than the Creator, who is blessed forever! Amen. (Rom 1:24–25)

The "therefore" indicates that the behavior about to be described is related to, and a result of, the idolatry. So, the question we must ask is: Was there a place in the ancient Roman world where people would engage in homosexual sex in the context of idol worship? And the answer, unsurprisingly, is yes.

Just like the ancient Egyptians and Canaanites, the early Greco-Roman world had many gods and goddesses, including Bacchus, Aphrodite, and Voluptas, who were worshiped through sexual sacrifice. Similar to Egypt and Canaan, ancient Roman law permitted same-sex sex between Roman men and slaves, prostitutes, and sometimes young people as a symbolic act of domination. Specifically, male Roman citizens were permitted to use both conquered men of other nations and young boys for sexual gratification, which is something that the Apostle Paul would have been familiar with as a member of a people who had been conquered and colonized by the Roman Empire.

In other words, the context of Romans 1 clearly indicates that the described sexual behavior isn't just "regular" consensual sexual intercourse or relationships between people of the same sex, but behavior in relation to either Roman idolatry and/or the immoral, exploitative behavior toward vulnerable populations that was permitted by Roman law. It is also clear that the people Paul is referring to in Romans 1 are *not Christians*—these are individuals who worship idols and not the one true God revealed in Jesus. Which raises the question of whether this passage has *any* applicability at all to LGBTQ Christians who enter into loving, committed same-sex relationships out of fidelity to their faith.

If you read the other "clobber passages" in Genesis, 1 Corinthians, 1 Timothy, and Jude in their literary contexts, every single chapter discusses some sort of same-sex sexual behavior that concerns *exploitation, idolatry,* and/or *cultural differences,* rather than offering an outright condemnation of the act of homosexual sex itself. Furthermore, there's not a single verse that condemns same-sex romantic relationships—all condemnations center on exploitative and idolatrous *sexual* behaviors rather than romantic partnerships.

There is obviously much more to say about each one of these passages: how the church has interpreted them historically and how an anti-LGBTQ posture became a hallmark of modern Christian ethics and theology. My book, *Queer & Christian: Reclaiming the Bible, Our Faith, and Our Place at the Table,* provides a deeper dive into these topics. But for our purposes here, this brief exploration of the biblical clobber passages helps us begin to see that, in fact, the Bible *is* clear in its condemnation in all six of the so-called clobber passages, condemning idolatry, sexual exploitation, and abuse. There is not a *single passage* where same-sex sex isn't mentioned in the context of idolatry, prostitution, or exploitation in the entirety of the Bible, and so to try to read modern notions of loving, consensual same-sex relationships into these ancient texts is to be unfaithful to the culture and context of the Scriptures themselves.

This seems to be a far timelier and convincing message that the church desperately needs to heed today, where sexual abuse continues to be a shockingly common occurrence. Instead of heeding the clear call of Scripture to reject sexual exploitation and abuse, Christians have far too often scapegoated the LGBTQ community using the very passages that were intended to protect the vulnerable from such abuse in the church. From a biblical perspective, there is no reason to believe that LGBTQ relationships or identities should be condemned by the church. In fact, I believe LGBTQ people and relationships should be celebrated as a unique expression and reflection of God's creativity and ever-expansive love, and can teach the church valuable lessons about the creativity and inclusivity of our God.

5

FRESH BIBLICAL INTERPRETATIONS

Jaime L. Waters, PhD

How should an LGBTQ person approach the Bible, especially when some of its texts have been used against them? In this chapter, I will attempt to answer this question by demonstrating four steps to reading Scripture and by highlighting Old Testament traditions that might inspire LGBTQ communities.

1. Read as you are and from where you are.
2. Lean into what resonates with you.
3. Pray with Scripture even if you critique it.
4. Study with liberation in mind, but recognize that not all texts are liberative.

These are recommendations I would give to anyone venturing into biblical study. Critically and prayerfully reading Scripture can be intellectually and spiritually enriching, but it is complicated and potentially damaging, especially for LGBTQ people.

The four steps listed above are an adapted *Lectio Divina* (reading, meditation, prayer, contemplation). These modifications offer a way to read Scripture thoughtfully, recognizing the importance of how we bring our whole selves to encounter God in its texts. The purpose of these steps is not to reach one definitive interpretation. Rather, they offer a way to engage Scripture, especially texts that can be difficult and problematic.

In this reflection, I will focus on portions of Genesis 19:1–38, the story of Sodom and Gomorrah, a potential "clobber passage." I recommend you read it in full, and I will draw attention to interpretive possibilities that might inspire rather than clobber. I will also recommend a few other Old Testament texts that might be more inspiring, especially for LGBTQ readers.

Read as you are and from where you are. I am an African American Catholic woman, biblical scholar, daughter, partner, friend, and ally to LGBTQ people. I bring these aspects of myself and more with me when I study and pray with Scripture. When I read Genesis 19, I am disturbed by its content and how its interpretation has harmed LGBTQ people. I am conscious of not wanting to promote harmful interpretations. It is important for readers to feel empowered and inspired to read in ways that will not promote hate.

Lean into what resonates with you. Not much in Genesis 19 resonates with me, and it is okay and important to say so. Not all texts are instructive or inspirational, even if we might want them to be. We can be selective when choosing texts for theological reflection. The lectionary is an example of such a selection process, and it is notable that most "clobber passages" are not proclaimed from the pulpit.

In Genesis 19, what resonates most with me is Lot's

hospitality. When Lot encounters the men/angels, he regards them as aliens to the land, and offers them respect, food, care, and shelter (see Gen 19:1–2). He treats them with dignity by washing their feet, which is a gesture of care, and by providing protection when their lives are threatened.

While there are problems in the text, some of which are discussed below, readers from LGBTQ communities might draw inspiration from the way that Lot interacts with the men/angels and the ways they rally together and protect themselves when under attack.

Pray with Scripture, even if you critique it. If I were praying with Genesis 19, I would offer thanks to God for giving me the time, space, and ability to reflect on the text. I would focus on those first two verses and think of ways that I might be more hospitable, especially to groups on the margins of society.

I would also pray with the problematic elements and interpretations. For instance, because the cities of Sodom and Gomorrah are depicted as wicked and because the men of the cities are criticized for their actions, Genesis 19 has been interpreted as biblical evidence against homosexuality, hence its "clobber" status.

The men are described saying, "Where are the men who came to you tonight? Bring them out to us, so that we may know them" (Gen 19:5). Lot characterizes their demand as wicked and instead offers his virgin daughters to the would-be rapists (Gen 19:7–8), as presumably this is a better option from his perspective.

Reading Genesis 19 as a statement against homosexuality is limited and ill-considered, as it fails to look at the larger literary context. Recall that Lot is within the tradition of Abraham and Sarah. In Genesis 18, Abraham and Sarah provide hospitality to the men before their visit to Lot, offering them a choice calf, cakes, and curds. Likewise, Abraham and Sarah face challenges and vulnerabilities as resident aliens. Abraham expresses concerns when he is in Egypt and Gerar, and he even puts Sarah in danger to protect himself, similar to Lot offering his daughters to protect the men (Gen 12:10–20; 20:1–18). Hospitality, survival in a foreign land, and exploitation of women are recurring themes in the Abrahamic narratives, and reflecting on those themes can offer a more informed approach to interpreting Genesis 19.

Knowing that this text has been and continues to be read in harmful ways, I would recommend that readers, especially LGBTQ readers, pray for those who have been injured by damaging interpretations of Genesis 19 and pray for the courage to work to protect and empower LGBTQ communities and consciously work against harmful readings.

Study with liberation in mind, but recognize that not all texts are liberative. When I read Genesis 19 for liberation, I read with the women of Sodom and Gomorrah and with Lot's daughters and wife. It is these nameless characters on the margins (or even missing from the narrative) who catch my eye.

For example, the women of Sodom and Gomorrah are not explicitly condemned, but they suffer the same fate as the men of the city. I take this as an example of how people on the margins can bear the brunt of suffering or experience hardships that are not their own creation. A liberative reading could use the text as a reminder to think from the experiences of those on the peripheries and work to promote justice for them.

Another liberative reading would be to draw attention to Lot's willingness to put his daughters in harm's way for the sake of his visitors. On the one hand, Lot's hospitality and protection of the angels seem admirable. Yet at the same time, by offering his daughters, Lot fails to protect these women for the sake of others. I am attentive to the parent-child dynamics in the text, ancient and modern ideas about fatherhood and daughterhood, and ways the daughters are depicted as expendable. The daughters get "justice" at the end of the narrative when they violate their father, giving him alcohol and raping him to continue the family line (Gen 19:30–38).

But a liberative reading of the rape of Lot should not be attempted, and an attempt to rationalize the daughters' actions could do harm to readers, especially victims and survivors of sexual assault.

Although we are reading Scripture, we should not feel compelled to justify any of the corruptions within it, nor the corrupt interpretations of it. It might be worthwhile to read the chapter as a literary creation whose purpose is not to speak on homosexuality at all, despite the insistence of some narrow-minded interpreters.

Genesis 19 offers a glimpse at how people, especially scribal elites in ancient Israel, thought about themselves vis-à-vis their neighbors. The narrative of Lot's daughters raping their father, for instance, serves as a corrupt origin story for Israel's cousin-neighbors, the Moabites and Ammonites, who are frequently enemies of the Israelites.

Likewise, the destruction of the Transjordan cities of Sodom and Gomorrah could foster an "us-versus-them" attitude between Israel and people living east of the Jordan River. The depiction of Israel's neighbors in a negative light might have political and theological motivations in antiquity, but it might also serve as good inspiration for readers today to work toward creating a less divisive society.

Having explored Genesis 19 with the adapted *Lectio Divina* in mind, what should we conclude? LGBTQ readers should recognize the power and perspective they bring to biblical interpretation. Understand and embrace the ways that social location, lived experiences, relationships, and faith commitments influence how you arrive at a text and what you draw from it. Another approach is to recognize the richness of tradition and explore other texts that are more affirming and encouraging.

MORE AFFIRMING OLD TESTAMENT TEXTS

The relationship between David and Jonathan is an example of a close, loving relationship between two men that is affirmed in Scripture. On multiple occasions, David and Jonathan are said to love one another, and they demonstrate their love publicly. "The soul of Jonathan was bound to the soul of David, and Jonathan loved him as his own soul" (1 Sam 18:1). The Hebrew word *nephesh* is translated as "soul," and it can also mean "life," "life force," or "breath." Each of these words emphasizes the depth of the connection between the two men. At the same time, the verb "to love" (*'ahab)* could suggest a romantic relationship; however, it is frequently used to suggest covenantal and political loyalty. Language of love is also common in ancient Near Eastern treaties to require or affirm fidelity.

Jonathan supports David politically even above his own father, Saul. When Saul plots to kill David because of his military successes, Jonathan alerts David and intercedes to convince his father not to attack David (1 Sam 19:1–7). When Jonathan dies in battle, David laments his death and performs multiple public signs of mourning (2 Sam 1:27).

The relationship between Ruth and Naomi is an example of a close, loving relationship between two women who support and care for one another after losing their husbands. Ruth clings (*dabaq*) to Naomi, using the same language associated with marriage, and the two women show love for one another throughout the Book of Ruth.

Scripture includes same-sex relationships in which people collaborate, support one another, and participate in liturgical activities. These relationships may not be explicitly or implicitly sexual, but they are intimate. They highlight cooperation, closeness, and partnership, themes that can speak to LGBTQ communities. Examples include Shiphrah and Puah (Exod 1:15–22), Elijah and Elisha (1 Kgs 19:11–21; 2 Kgs 2:1–18), Judith and her maidservant (Jdt 10–13), Miriam and other women singing and performing liturgical dance (Exod 15:20–21), and women performing ritual lament and instruction (Jer 9:17–22).

The prophet Jeremiah is commanded not to marry or have children (Jer 16:1–4), his life symbolically reflecting the desolation and lack of viability at his time. Yet Jeremiah has close relationships with friends Baruch, his scribe (Jer 36, 43, 45), and Ebed-Melech, a eunuch who saves Jeremiah's life (Jer 38–39).

Praying with these texts, rather than the clobber passages, can be lifegiving and encouraging, affirming dynamic and intimate same-sex relationships and helping LGBTQ readers encounter God in Scripture.

6

GOD'S EMANCIPATORY EMBRACE

Walter Brueggemann, PhD

After the memory of Moses, the daring of David, and the opulence of Solomon, ancient Israel came to believe that it was God's chosen people who had a monopoly on God's love and God's goodness.

In the eighth century BCE, the prophet Amos took as his work helping his contemporaries in Israel to see that Israel, in its chosenness, had no monopoly on God's goodness. Its chosenness was no pass from obedience to God's rule and no guarantee of God's love.

Thus, in his oracles against the nations, Amos shows, one by one, that Israel's neighbors and adversaries were subject to God's rule and judgment (Amos 1—2). Surprisingly, he also includes Judah (2:4–5) and Israel (2:6–11) among those called to harsh account by God.

And then, in one of his most remarkable utterances, Amos asks:

Are you not like the Ethiopians to me,
O people of Israel? says the LORD.
Did I not bring Israel up from the land of Egypt
and the Philistines from Caphtor and the Arameans
from Kir? (Amos 9:7)

Israel remembered its emancipation from slavery under Pharaoh in Egypt, and imagined that God's exodus deliverance of Israel was a singular act, without parallel in the history of the world. After all, God had identified Israel as "my firstborn son" (Exod 4:22). But Amos insisted otherwise. He asks of Israel two rhetorical questions.

Yes, YHWH did *bring up* the Philistines from Caphtor.

Yes, YHWH did *bring up* the Arameans (Syrians) from Kir.

Amos names two foreign peoples that were at different times Israel's most threatening enemies: the Philistines and later the Syrians. He dares to say that God enacts "exoduses" for Israel's enemies. He affirms that God's emancipatory power extends to other peoples who are not commonly taken to be "chosen."

He debunks Israel's claim to the exclusionary love and justice of God and insists that, in its universal scope, YHWH's emancipatory reach extends everywhere, at many times, and in many places, bringing emancipation for those not yet liberated. Indeed, he suggests that the wide sweep of history under YHWH is a sequence of exoduses, so that there is nothing exclusionary about Israel's emancipatory memory or claim.

Thus we may consider an inventory of *the chosen* and *the unchosen* whom God emancipates. The chosen and unchosen emancipated by God might be any of the following:

a) *Israel* has no doubt that it was "the chosen people," but now Amos says that even Israel's enemies are subject to YHWH's emancipatory intention.

b) *White people,* in our modern world, often take themselves to be God's chosen people. Thus white European culture is then seen as the most "advanced" with its colonial exploitation and its mastery in arts, science, and wealth. And now Amos, to the contrary, dares to say that people of color (represented by the Ethiopians) are also subject to God's emancipatory love. God's love is not exclusively for white people, even though Europeans who came to America took their whiteness as a privileged status and had few qualms about imitating Pharaoh in enslaving people of color.

c) For much too long, it has been easy to say that *males* believe they too are God's chosen people. They are the ones with power who have been able to shape history and accumulate wealth. They are the ones for whom the verbs *exploit, conquer, occupy, possess* most readily apply. And then the prophetic tradition, extended and enacted through the testimony and ministry of Jesus, showed that God's emancipatory love reached effectively toward females. Thus Mary Magdalene was among the earliest disciples of Jesus. And the Apostle Paul can declare that in Christ "there is no longer male and female" (Gal 3:28). The gender revolution continues as women are increasingly welcomed into the public life of the world, and even, belatedly, into the ministry of the church.

d) Anyone can see that *straight persons* also believe that they are the chosen of God, who have been able to define social power and social acceptability. Anyone who deviates from the straight

> world has been excluded forever from social acceptance, has been deemed a danger and a threat to social wellbeing, and thus subject to harsh treatment. And now, belatedly, we can see that the reach of God's emancipatory love extends beyond straight people, who are readily approved by society, to include LGBTQ persons, who have been held much too long in the bondage of social censorship and social disapproval. The passion of God's emancipatory embrace goes well beyond straight people.

God will not be contained.

We can see, historically, that these several emancipatory concerns have come to fruition very slowly and to some extent in sequence:

First, *Gentiles* beyond chosen Israel;

then *people of color* beyond whites;

later, *females* beyond males;

and very belatedly, *LGBTQ persons* beyond straight hegemony.

But it has happened and continues to happen in all these traditions! God's truth is marching on! We are discerning that God's love, justice, freedom, mercy, and faithfulness cannot be contained in our self-imagined categories of chosenness and privilege. Our several orthodoxies of nationalism, racism, sexism, and gender exclusion all have imagined a God who could be safely kept in our preferred boundaries.

But *the God of the covenant,* who is *the God of the gospel,* will not be so contained. Indeed, it is evident that God's peculiar attentiveness is especially drawn toward those who are regularly denied legitimacy in our social arrangements.

We can knowingly speak of "God's preferential option" not only for the poor, but toward all those who are otherwise discounted.

It seems clear that all such efforts to "box in" the God of freedom are grounded in fear. We imagine that the "other"—the ones unlike us—are a threat, and so we fashion exclusionary practices and rules. It turns out, however, that such fear is not the last word. God intends all of us who see ourselves as chosen—whites, males, straight—to see that faith, hope, and love are stronger than fear and will prevail.

And so the other need not be a threat, but can be welcomed as a neighbor.

Because the reach of emancipation toward LGBTQ persons is the latest such move toward liberation, we may pay special attention to the way it sounds through the lines of Amos:

> Are you not like the LGBTQ persons to me, O straights?
> Yes!
> Did I not bring up straight people to be emancipated
> agents in the world? Yes!
> And did I not bring up LGBTQ persons to first class
> citizenship in the world? Yes!
> And did I not bring up LGBTQ persons to be free for
> a life of joy and freedom and well-being in the
> world? Yes!

Like the earlier questions posed by Amos, these world-shattering questions of Amos require a vigorous yes in response. It is a yes of gospel emancipation. It is a yes of limitless love. It is a yes of well-being that counters all our fearful exclusions.

Amos could not have been popular among the "chosen" for such an utterance. That, however, is not much against his bold truth-telling. The good news summons us to a vigorous, unafraid yes toward all those whom the Pharaohs of the world continue to keep in bondage. As the Apostle Paul concludes: "For freedom Christ has set us free. Stand firm, therefore, and do not submit again to a yoke of slavery" (Gal 5:1).

7

THE STORY OF SODOM AND GOMORRAH

Richard J. Clifford, SJ

Most of us know the Old Testament from brief excerpts. We seldom have the time for extended passages, still less for entire biblical books. It's good to read the Bible, of course, but snippets alone can deprive us of the contexts that provide depth. The Bible often communicates its message through stories, which require lots of space.

An example of the danger of cursory reading is Genesis 19:1–11, the attack of the men of Sodom on the two angelic servants sent to protect Lot and his family. For centuries, interpretation has been overdetermined by the name of the town where the incident took place, Sodom, which has given us the name of the sexual act, sodomy. Dictionaries routinely define sodomy as "sexual intercourse involving anal or oral copulation."

Frank and accurate, to be sure, but terribly misleading as a label for a single scene in a story that's seventy-one verses long, beginning with Abraham in chapter 18 and ending with

Lot in chapter 19. The one-dimensional label keeps readers from appreciating the whole story.

THE CONTEXT OF GENESIS

Readers should take account of the context of all the Genesis stories and compare them to other episodes in the book. A good example of meaning deepened by context is Genesis 22:1–14, where God commands Abraham to sacrifice his son Isaac, for whom he long waited. Like Genesis 19, this episode is misunderstood if we read it without considering similar divine commands.

The shocking command in Genesis 22 is not unique. God's command to Abraham near the end of the larger story to *give up* his son Isaac echoes his command at the beginning of the saga to *give up* his homeland (Gen 12:1). To emphasize the parallel, Genesis 22 reprises the earlier command from 12:1 ("Go...to the land that I will show you"), saying, "go to the land of Moriah...on one of the mountains that I shall show you" (Gen 22:2). The parallel commands make it clear that Abraham must be ready to surrender to God what he most values—his homeland and his beloved son—to receive them back as God's gift.

The theme of a father giving up his beloved son appears two more times in Genesis. In chapter 38, Judah gives up his only son, Selah, to Tamar; in chapter 43, Jacob gives up Benjamin, the remaining son of Rachel, by allowing him to go to Egypt. Both fathers receive back their sons along with other gifts. The explanatory value of the contexts from Genesis 12 and 22 reminds us to appreciate the connections between Genesis 18 and 19.

ABRAHAM CONTRASTED WITH LOT

Returning to Genesis 18—19, we note that almost from the beginning of the Abraham saga (chapters 12—25), the patriarch is contrasted with Lot, his nephew. Both men are married, but their prospects of continuing the family line differ decidedly. Lot, young and already with children, is by any natural standard the right choice to continue the family line. Abraham is seventy-five, and his wife Sarah long ago passed childbearing age (18:11).

In the hidden purpose of God, however, Abraham and Sarah will become the parents of Isaac, the promised child. Lot, alas, will turn out to be "the nephew from hell," forever requiring his uncle's bailouts and rescues. For example, when both men's flocks grow beyond the pastureland's capacity to feed them, Abraham exercises his authority as family head in a surprisingly generous way. He invites Lot to choose any pastureland he wants: "If you take the left hand, then I will go to the right, or if you take the right hand, then I will go to the left" (Gen 13:9).

Lot, of course, should have deferred to his uncle, but he instead looked across the Jordan River to the Jordan plain, at that time green and abundantly watered, leaving the land of Canaan to settle in the city of Sodom. (Its exact location is unknown, but located somewhere in the area of the southern Dead Sea.)

Unfortunately, the Jordan plain turned into a war zone fought over by two coalitions of petty kings. The victorious coalition seized Sodom, and Lot's family was among the captured. Word of his nephew's capture reached Abraham, who marched out with 328 of his men to rescue Lot and recover his possessions.

When the victorious Abraham returned, a local king, Melchizedek of Salem (another name for Jerusalem, meaning "peace" in Hebrew) celebrated his victory and blessed "God Most High, who has delivered your enemies into your hand!" (Gen 14:20). Abraham, however, refused to take the spoils of his victory (to which he had a perfect right) lest anyone say, "I have made Abram rich" (Gen 14:23).

Time passed. Lot had two daughters, while Abraham and Sarah had only hope for the promised child. Then, at noon on a blistering day at Mamre, south of Jerusalem, Abraham dozing at the entrance to his tent awoke to find three men standing before him. Awed by their presence, he rushed to welcome them with extravagant hospitality. His wife and his servants joined.

Two of the men turned out to be angels, and the third was revealed very gradually to be the Lord himself. (The number of men, three, probably reflected the popular belief that a god was typically accompanied by two angelic servants.)

During the elaborate meal that Abraham served them, the Lord promised, "At the set time I will return to you, in due season, and Sarah shall have a son" (Gen 18:14). Abraham and Sarah laughed in delight (Hebrew *ṣāḥaq*) at the prospect of a son within the year.

As the three men rose to leave, accompanied by Abraham, they looked down at Sodom, Lot's city in the distant plain. The two servants peeled off to journey to Sodom, leaving Abraham alone with the Lord. In an intimate and tender reflection, the Lord recalled his promise that Abraham would become a mighty nation in whom all the nations of the earth would find blessing.

Then, thinking perhaps of the victims of Sodom's wicked inhabitants, the Lord reflected: "How great is the outcry against Sodom and Gomorrah and how very grave their sin! I must go down and see whether they have done altogether according to the outcry that has come to me, and if not, I will know" (Gen 18:20–21).

Abraham correctly guessed that the Lord would punish Sodom severely. Here was an exceptional opportunity for Abraham to rescue his nephew from the impending destruction. Relying on the promise that he would bring blessing to the nations, and aware of his responsibility for his kinsman, Abraham asked the Lord: "Will you indeed sweep away the righteous with the wicked? Suppose there are fifty righteous within the city; will you then sweep away the place and not forgive it for the fifty righteous who are in it?...Shall not the Judge of all the earth do what is just?" (Gen 18:23–25).

With tact and boldness, Abraham succeeded in persuading God not to destroy the entire city for the sake of as few as ten righteous (Gen 18:32). Lot's family will be fewer than ten, though even those few will fall short by disregarding the messengers' command to leave the city before it was destroyed (Gen 19:12–23).

AVOIDING MISINTERPRETATIONS

Genesis 19:1–11 has given rise to a misinterpretation of the entire story: the encounter of two angelic visitors with Lot and the citizens of the city. Though Lot is not a full citizen of the doomed city (Gen 19:9), neither he nor his family behave righteously, for they accept only grudgingly the angels' directives meant to save them.

Moreover, Lot's reception of the angelic visitors suffers in comparison with Abraham's reception of the Lord. Abraham rushes to serve them an extravagant meal and involves his wife and servants, whereas Lot welcomes them alone with what seems to be an ordinary meal.

After the meal in Lot's house, "The men of Sodom, both

young and old, all the people to the last man, surrounded the house; and they called to Lot" to bring his two guests into the town square to be gang-raped (Gen 19:4–5). Conscious to a foolish extreme of his role as host, Lot offers the mob a shocking counteroffer: "I have two daughters who have not known a man; let me bring them out to you, and do to them as you please; only do nothing to these men, for they have come under the shelter of my roof" (19:8). The mob scorns his proposal and moves closer to break down the door.

Given our interest not to allow the terms *Sodom* and *sodomy* to take over our interpretation, it is important to note that Lot's offer to surrender his two daughters to the mob's lust implicitly reveals his own take on what the men of Sodom really intended.

In Lot's eyes, the men of Sodom were not intent on homosexual rape specifically, but rather on humiliating Lot, whom they despised as an immigrant (19:9), and his two guests. Recent accounts of warfare make clear that systematic sexual assault on noncombatants is an all-too-common means of demoralizing and defeating enemies. Lot's words seem to indicate he is referring to that very practice.

Lot's two guests rescue him by pulling him back into the house and shutting the door. The guests rescue the host! When the messengers tell Lot to lead his sons-in-law out of the doomed city, they laugh off his warnings. The passage uses the same Hebrew verb—*ṣāḥaq*—that describes Abraham and Sarah expressing delight at the prospect of a son. Even Lot, along with his two daughters, "lingered" (19:16), and the messengers had to seize them and lead them out of the city by the hand.

Once outside the city, Lot delays leaving for the safety of the hills using an excuse so foolish that it must be a humorous putdown of Lot. He asks the messengers permission to go to a little town, Zoar (Hebrew *ṣō'ār*, "small"). Does Lot think that a small town would escape God's notice? The silly excuse seems to echo the lighthearted interplay between Sarah and the Lord in Abraham's tent (Gen 18:11–15).

Here, however, Lot's foolish behavior displays his inability to care for his family. Lot's folly extends even to his wife who, despite warnings, looked back at the rain of sulfur and fire and turned into a pillar of salt (19:26)—the kind visible even today on the southern shores of the Dead Sea.

THE FUNDAMENTAL MESSAGE

There is one last reference to Abraham in Genesis 19:27: "And he looked down toward Sodom and Gomorrah and toward all the land of the Plain and saw the smoke of the land going up like the smoke of a furnace." What was he thinking as he looked? We are not told, just as we are not told what Abraham was thinking in chapter 22 when he walked with Isaac toward the mountain to sacrifice him. Abraham's silence in both instances is a reminder that the Bible leaves much unsaid, inviting the reader to imagine the thoughts of the characters.

The final episode of Lot's story comes in Genesis 19:30–38, when Lot's two daughters, whose husbands were apparently killed in the destruction, attempt to beget children through incestuous unions with their father. They take revenge on their father for exposing them to the mob's lust. Getting him drunk, they lie with him on successive nights. The firstborn daughter's son was Moab, the ancestor of the Moabites, and the younger daughter's son was Ben-ammi, the ancestor of the Ammonites.

It can hardly escape readers' notice that the daughters' immoral and aggressive actions contrast totally with the faith and obedience of Abraham and Sarah.

In conclusion, the sexual assault on the two angelic servants is certainly not a warning against homosexuality, and all attempts to interpret the narrative in that direction seriously misread the story. Instead, the story gives us a memorable portrait of Abraham and his wife in contrast to Abraham's nephew, Lot. It displays Abraham's ability to bring God's blessings to the nations, offer hospitality to strangers, care for his family, and live trustingly by God's promise.

8

SODOM AND GOMORRAH AND OUR INHOSPITALITY

Grant Hartley

For much of my early life, I was under the impression that the destruction of Sodom and Gomorrah in Genesis 19 was an expression of God's wrath against people like me: gay people. I was subtly encouraged to feel little for the wicked inhabitants of those cities, even as, inwardly, I saw myself in them.

Consequently, I felt that I could never let anyone know what I was experiencing. I wondered if God was angry with me because of feelings I could not control or erase, no matter how much I tried. I wondered if God wanted to destroy me.

Vital lessons from the passage went over my head because I had misunderstood it to be about gay people. But a deeper look at the story reveals a message that all of us desperately need to hear.

Years after coming out in college, I have discovered just

how much the story must teach us about God's righteous anger toward arrogance and violence, and about his abundant hospitality toward us despite our weakness and failure.

To see this more clearly, the passage must be examined in its larger context. The real beginning for this episode is in chapter 18, when three angels in the form of three men appear to Abraham "as he sat at the entrance of his tent in the heat of the day" (Gen 18:1).

Abraham's response to the angels reveals him to be an exceptional host. He brings out water to wash their feet after their long journey and rushes off to prepare a feast. He tells his wife, Sarah, to prepare cakes, slaughters a young calf, and offers them milk and rich cheese.

Through the angels, God delivers a message to the elderly couple: Sarah will give birth to a son at the same time next year. The two struggle to believe—Sarah even fails to contain her laughter and is gently rebuked—but finally, they accept the angelic message. Just before the guests leave, God reveals to Abraham his plans to destroy Sodom and Gomorrah, a city of extreme wickedness. An initial contrast is set up here between Abraham's hospitality and the unnamed "sin of Sodom."

Abraham is distraught over the fate of the cities, where he knows his nephew, Lot, is currently living; his care for the stranger extends to the inhabitants of the cities of the plain.

> Will you indeed sweep away the righteous with the wicked? Suppose there are fifty righteous within the city; will you then sweep away the place and not forgive it for the fifty righteous who are in it? Far be it from you to do such a thing, to slay the righteous with the wicked, so that the righteous fare as the wicked! (Gen 18:23–25)

God graciously agrees to relent for the sake of fifty righteous people. But Abraham does not stop there—he bargains with God until the number is reduced to a mere ten. However, the reader soon discovers that even the drastically reduced number is not met.

Two of the angels then travel directly to Sodom to rescue Lot, who greets them at the city gate. Attempting to be a good host himself, and aware of how dangerous the city could become at night, Lot urges them to stay at his own house rather than in the city square.

Lot prepares a feast as well, but interestingly, the only food explicitly mentioned in the text is "unleavened bread." Before anyone in the house lies down to sleep, a crowd arrives. "The men of the city, the men of Sodom, both young and old, all the people to the last man" arrive at the front door and demand to rape the honored guests (Gen 19:4–5). The fact that every single man from the city makes this demand suggests that this is not a group of gay men. What kind of city, in the ancient world or in any time and place, would have had an entirely gay population?

The emphasis is clearly on violent humiliation, not sexual intimacy or pleasure. The men of Sodom wish to brutalize the angels, not seduce them. What could be the motivation for wanting to humiliate the angels in this way?

Lot, for all his attempts at being a good host, utterly fails as a father when he offers the men his own young daughters instead. "Look, I have two daughters who have not known a man; let me bring them out to you, and do to them as you please; only do nothing to these men, for they have come under the shelter of my roof" (Gen 19:8).

Lot fails to make his house safe for his own children—*this too is an act of inhospitality*. We get further insight into the character and motivation of these men in their response to Lot's offer. They deride him for being a foreigner in their city and threaten to rape him. These are not gay men looking for a good time with out-of-towners. This is a hateful, violent mob.

The angels miraculously disperse the crowd with a blinding flash of light and command Lot to gather his family and flee first thing in the morning. Lot attempts to round them up that night, and only his wife and daughters wish to go with him. But even after the dawn breaks, Lot fails to act decisively. Graciously, the angels grab Lot and his family by the hand and drag them to safety outside the city gate. Lot seems maddeningly ambivalent about leaving, but God nonetheless rescues him and his family from destruction.

Before leaving, the angels enjoin them to flee to the hills without looking back, and in an echo of Abraham's bargaining with God to spare Sodom and Gomorrah, Lot bargains with the angels to allow him and his family to flee to the nearby town of Zoar instead.

The comparison is striking: Abraham bargains for mercy on the inhabitants of the cities, while Lot bargains for mercy for himself; Abraham bargains for God to relent, while Lot bargains for God to ease his escape. As they flee, Lot's wife, perhaps identifying with the wicked cities, turns back one final time, and turns into a pillar of salt.

The episode concludes by returning to Abraham:

> Abraham went early in the morning to the place where he had stood before the Lord; and he looked down toward Sodom and Gomorrah and toward all the land of the Plain and saw the smoke of the land going up like the smoke of a furnace. So it was that, when God destroyed the cities of the Plain, God remembered Abraham, and sent Lot out of the midst of the overthrow, when he overthrew the cities in which Lot had settled. (Gen 19:27–29)

With this full context in mind, the meaning of the destruction of Sodom and Gomorrah is summed up by the prophet Ezekiel: they "had pride, excess of food, and prosperous ease, but did not aid the poor and needy"—including the angels, who should have been honored guests. "They were haughty, and did abominable things before me"—arriving in a violent mob to gang rape visitors. "Therefore I removed them when I saw it"—the inhospitality and disregard for foreign guests.

As followers of Christ, we know that by practicing hospitality, "some have entertained angels without knowing it," as the author of Hebrews tells us (Heb 13:2). John writes that "we love because he first loved us" (1 John 4:19). Likewise, we invite others into our family because we have been invited into the family of God. Jesus makes it clear that what is done for "the least of these who are members of my family" is in a real sense done for him (Matt 25:40).

Our faith demands hospitality of us, especially toward the poor, the needy, and the stranger.

Using the story of Sodom and Gomorrah to suggest God's wrath against gay people makes it easy to avoid its actual demands to open our wallets, homes, and hearts to people in need. How many times has misunderstanding, empowered by hatred of the other, led some to use this passage to sanction everything that made Sodom guilty: kicking children out of their homes, refusing to serve certain people, discriminating in housing and jobs, breaking families apart, and fighting against civil rights?

If one were trying to relieve oneself of this passage's radical demands of hospitality, twisting the story to focus on gay people would be a convenient strategy.

But as important as that message is, stopping there would keep us from the other, deeper, point of the story: God's gracious hospitality toward us. God is obviously under no obligation to bargain with human beings, but he allows Abraham to haggle with him to save Sodom and Gomorrah. When even a handful are not found, God sets out to save Lot and his family from destruction. When Lot hesitates instead of taking decisive action, God drags them all to safety, and even puts up with Lot's complaining after the fact.

God's call for us to show hospitality to the poor, the needy, and the stranger is naturally connected to seeing ourselves as poor, needy strangers to whom God displays hospitality, despite our weakness and even our resistance.

We show hospitality to others because God has shown immense hospitality to us. Our motivation for opening our wallets, homes, and hearts to the poor, the needy, and the stranger must not merely be a sense of guilt. We offer hospitality out of an overflow of the riches we have already been given by God.

I invite you to see yourself in the story of the destruction of Sodom and Gomorrah. I invite you to see yourself as an inhabitant of the cities, not because the story is about some divine wrath against gay people, but because a propensity toward inhospitality, pride, violence, and selfishness is within all of us.

But I also invite you to see yourself in Lot, an inhabitant of the city who was saved. I invite you to consider that even when we fall short of the demands of hospitality, even when we fail in loving the poor and needy, God is gracious and hospitable, willing and able to drag us to safety and invite us into his family.

9

THE CONTEXT OF NEW TESTAMENT PASSAGES ON HOMOSEXUALITY

Harold W. Attridge, PhD

Several New Testament passages often cited in discussions of the Christian assessment of same-sex relations present two sets of issues: what the text originally meant and what role they might play in constructing a contemporary ethical stance.[1]

ROMANS 1:26–27

Without a doubt, the most prominent text is part of Paul's Letter to the Romans, but the verses need to be cited in this larger context:

1. Due to the specificity of language, this chapter preserves the New American Bible (Revised Edition).

> While claiming to be wise, they became fools and exchanged the glory of the immortal God for the likeness of an image of mortal man or of birds or of four-legged animals or of snakes.
>
> Therefore, God handed them over to impurity through the lusts of their hearts for the mutual degradation of their bodies. They exchanged the truth of God for a lie and revered and worshiped the creature rather than the creator, who is blessed forever. Amen. Therefore, God handed them over to degrading passions. Their females exchanged natural relations for unnatural, and the males likewise gave up natural relations with females and burned with lust for one another. Males did shameful things with males and thus received in their own persons the due penalty for their perversity. And since they did not see fit to acknowledge God, God handed them over to their undiscerning mind to do what is improper. They are filled with every form of wickedness, evil, greed, and malice; full of envy, murder, rivalry, treachery, and spite. They are gossips and scandalmongers and they hate God. They are insolent, haughty, boastful, ingenious in their wickedness, and rebellious toward their parents. They are senseless, faithless, heartless, ruthless. Although they know the just decree of God that all who practice such things deserve death, they not only do them but give approval to those who practice them. (Rom 1:22–32)

The larger context reminds us that Paul's overall argument in this section of Romans is that all human beings are sinful and in need of the righteousness that God has freely given to all, through the faith that Christ inaugurated. To make his point, Paul first deploys what is probably boilerplate Jewish rhetoric denouncing the wickedness of the Gentile world.

Paul will soon turn the tables and declare those who make this claim to be guilty of sin as well, but here he uses their rhetoric. He is not analyzing the principles of proper sexual behavior or examining its variety. He is following in the familiar footsteps of powerful Jewish critics of the Gentile world.

Paul's rhetoric polemicizes against idolatry, arguing that those who worship idols have been abandoned by God to their most base desires and practices. "They are filled with every form of wickedness, evil, greed, and malice; full of envy, murder, rivalry, treachery, and spite" (Rom 1:29). This is not ethical analysis—it is a prophetic denunciation.

In its focus on the role of "degrading passions" (1:26), Paul's language reflects the influence of Stoic moralizing, which sharply contrasted reasoned, moral behavior with irrational emotional drives that gain control over the human self. The critique turns first to sexual behavior involving "unnatural" activity, a judgment that continues to reflect Stoic moralizing.

Paul declaims: "Their females exchanged natural relations for unnatural, and the males likewise gave up natural relations with females and burned with lust for one another." Paul clearly denounces same-sex behavior, while he does not explain exactly why it is "unnatural." He probably does not have in mind the kind of "natural law" thinking that would later emerge in Catholic moral theology.

It may be debated whether the judgment about the morality of sexual behavior, according to natural law theory, is correct. According to that theory, the "ends" of particular actions are determined by the Creator. The end, or *telos*, of human sexual activity is twofold: to unite the human beings who engage in it and to produce offspring.

In official Catholic teaching, both of those ends must be at least possible for a sexual act to be moral. Hence same-sex activity, which cannot end in reproduction, is deemed immoral, as is artificial contraception. Many people would question that reasoning, even if one assumes the premise that moral ends are built into the created order.

Why do both "ends" of a sexual act have to be present to guarantee its moral character? Certainly, in the case of artificial contraception, the *sensus fidelium* is that it is not immoral.

Whatever one may think of natural law reasoning, it is not what Paul pursues. Rather, he works with an untested assumption that same-sex attraction and activity is not to be found among other animals. Other first-century moralists influenced by Cynic and Stoic traditions made similar appeals. Should a contemporary Catholic ethic of sexuality be grounded in such a set of assumptions? I hope not.

Paul, and the Jewish preaching that inspired this passage of Romans, may have objected to certain kinds of same-sex behavior on grounds that most moderns would share. Coerced and exploitative sexual relations were no doubt a feature of many same-sex relations in Paul's world. Such concerns need to be explicitly articulated and addressed in developing an ethic of sexual relations.

1 CORINTHIANS 6:9–10

Paul writes First Corinthians from Ephesus to a community he founded, to answer questions about controversial issues. In the process, he offers guidance and admonitions about behavior, as he does in chapter 6. In the previous chapter, Paul had addressed a particular case of improper behavior: a man marrying his stepmother.

He then chides the Corinthians for engaging in lawsuits against one another—not what members of the Body of Christ do! These specific cases lead to a more general admonition about proper moral behavior, which is required for salvation.

> Do you not know that the unjust will not inherit the kingdom of God? Do not be deceived; neither fornicators nor idolaters nor adulterers nor boy prostitutes nor sodomites nor thieves nor the greedy nor drunkards nor slanderers nor robbers will inherit the kingdom of God. That is what some of you used to be; but now you have had yourselves washed, you were sanctified, you were justified in the name of the Lord Jesus Christ and in the Spirit of our God. (1 Cor 6:9–11)

The bottom line is to remind the Corinthians that they have been sanctified through their baptism and that, in their new life, they need to avoid things recognized as immoral. As was true in Romans, Paul's admonition is not an analysis of ethical principles nor an application of general norms to specific cases. It assumes agreed-upon vices and sins that are to be avoided.

Most of these are clear enough: theft, greed, drunkenness, and slander are incompatible with membership in the body of Christ. Paul begins with several sexual matters, some of which are also clear; fornication and adultery are to be avoided, along with idolatry. But then he uses two words, *malakoi* and *arsenokoitai,* literally "softies" and "male bedders," whose meanings have been much debated.

The New American Bible translations, "boy prostitutes"

and "sodomites," offer one set of options. Many more have been considered, including "effeminate" and "abusers of themselves with mankind" from the King James Version, and "male prostitutes" and "men who engage in illicit sex" from the Revised Standard Version.

Exactly what behaviors Paul has in mind is not clear. Again, the first-century environment should not be forgotten, in which prostitution was not uncommon, forced sexual relations with enslaved people was a fact of life, and pederasty, although often condemned, was enshrined in classic sources (e.g., Plato's *Symposium*). This is not a thoughtful analysis of human sexual orientation or activity, but a standard denunciation of Gentile immorality.

1 TIMOTHY 1:10

Another list of vices appears in 1 Timothy 1:10, a letter probably written in Paul's name by a disciple. The context, like the two earlier texts, sketches an extensive vice list:

> We know that the law is good, provided that one uses it as law, with the understanding that law is meant not for a righteous person but for the lawless and unruly, the godless and sinful, the unholy and profane, those who kill their fathers or mothers, murderers, the unchaste, sodomites, kidnappers, liars, perjurers, and whatever else is opposed to sound teaching, according to the glorious gospel of the blessed God, with which I have been entrusted. (1 Tim 1:8–11)

Two sex-related words appear at the beginning of verse 10: *pornoi* and *arsenoikoitai*. The first, which the NABRE renders "the unchaste," is related to the word for "prostitute" and is the root of the word "pornography." The generic translation of "the unchaste" captures the broad denunciation of inappropriate sexual behavior.

The second word, "male bedders," which also appears in 1 Corinthians, is too narrowly translated as "practicing homosexuals." Male behavior is in view, but the precise issue is as uncertain here, as in Paul's genuine letter.

JUDE 6–7

One final text is sometimes brought into the discussion of the New Testament and the ethics of same-sex activity. The Letter of Jude, attributed to a disciple who was probably a relative of Jesus (see Matt 13:55; Mark 6:3) and a brother of the James who probably wrote the Letter of James.

The brief letter of Jude offers a general warning against false teachers, described as "godless persons, who pervert the grace of our God into licentiousness and who deny our only Master and Lord, Jesus Christ" (Jude 4). These teachers are then compared to biblical villains:

> The angels too, who did not keep to their own domain but deserted their proper dwelling, he has kept in eternal chains, in gloom, for the judgment of the great day. Likewise, Sodom, Gomorrah, and the surrounding towns, which, in the same manner as they, indulged in sexual promiscuity and practiced unnatural vice, serve as an example by undergoing a punishment of eternal fire. (Jude 6–7)

The first comparison is the "fallen angels," who, according to the legend of Genesis 6, had intercourse with human women. The second comparison is to the people of Sodom and Gomorrah, who, according to Genesis 19, attempted to assault two angels sent by God to visit Lot in Sodom.

The locals were duly punished with sulfur and fire (Gen 19:24) for their crime. Although the Sodomites gave their name to sinful sexual behavior, their major fault was not respecting Lot's guests. The phrases referring to the sin of the cities of Sodom and Gomorrah emphasize the sexual dimension of their action.

The first, *ekporneusasai,* recalls the *pornoi* of 1 Timothy 1:10, and is appropriately translated as "engage in sexual promiscuity." The second phrase, *apelthousai opiso sarkos eteras,* is literally "going after other flesh," which captures some of the violent aggression in the action condemned.

Violent, coerced sex of any kind is never acceptable. All readers can agree on that principle, whatever assumptions about sexual behavior lie behind these two verses of Jude.

SCRIPTURE AND CONTEMPORARY SEXUAL ETHICS

None of the biblical texts mentioning sexual immorality provides a general framework for thinking about sexual ethics. As noted in connection with Romans, the language of what is "natural" does appear, but that language has little relationship to theories of natural law.

All these passages in the New Testament reflect the condemnation of immorality that was part of a Jewish (and then a Christian) critique of contemporary culture. There were in the first century, as there are today, sexual practices, especially violent and coercive sexual engagement, that deserved negative judgment by readers of Scripture and anyone else with a sound moral compass.

Yet the general framework for thinking about sexual morality should not be determined by generalized condemnations of undefined behavior. Our sexual ethics should be more nuanced and sensitive, and grounded in the command to love, as all Christian ethics should be.

10

SAINT PAUL ON HOMOSEXUALITY

Thomas D. Stegman, SJ

Therefore God gave them up in the lusts of their hearts to impurity, to the degrading of their bodies among themselves, because they exchanged the truth about God for a lie and worshiped and served the creature rather than the Creator, who is blessed forever! Amen.

For this reason God gave them up to degrading passions. Their women exchanged natural intercourse for unnatural, and in the same way also the men, giving up natural intercourse with women, were consumed with passion for one another. Men committed shameless acts with men and received in their own persons the due penalty for their error.

And since they did not see fit to acknowledge God, God gave them up to a debased mind and to things that should not be done. They were filled with every kind of wickedness, evil, covetousness, malice. Full of envy, murder, strife, deceit, craftiness, they are gossips, slanderers, God-haters, insolent, haughty, boastful, inventors of evil, rebellious toward parents, foolish, faithless, heartless, ruthless. They know God's decree,

> that those who practice such things deserve to die—yet they not only do them but even applaud others who practice them.
>
> Rom 1:24–32

Romans 1:26–27 is frequently cited as Paul's blanket condemnation of homosexuality. Careful exegesis calls into question this unnuanced view. I point this out in my commentary in *The Paulist Biblical Commentary*, which I share here.

In response to the Gentiles' choice to worship creatures instead of the Creator, Paul declares three times that "God gave them over"—to unruly desires in their hearts (v. 24), to dishonorable passions (v. 26), and to a base mind (v. 28). Abandonment of God results in the *entire* person being adversely affected. There is a progression from disordered passions to calculated insolence that rips apart the fabric of the human community.

First, Paul states that God gave Gentiles over to "desires" (my translation). While sexual lusts are primarily intended, *epithymia* has a broader reference. The rejection of God as the source of life meant that people sought "life" in futile ways, following their sordid inclinations. In doing so, they distorted and damaged the image of God they were created to embody. Rather than grow in the ways of holiness, they fell into "impurity."

Second, Paul turns to homosexual relations as an example of the type of behavior to which God handed over people. Those who exchanged worship of the living God for idols then exchanged "natural intercourse for unnatural."

Paul comes from a religious tradition that forbids same-sex relations (cf. Lev 18:22; 20:13). Like many Jews of his day, he regarded such relations as a quintessential vice among Gentiles. This example, in his view, illustrates another instance of the distortion of God's image (cf. "male and female" in Gen 1:27).

Paul's negative example of same-sex relations is an oft-cited text, one that calls for careful interpretation. On the one hand, there is little doubt that he viewed homosexual relations as "unnatural" and contrary to God's law.

On the other hand, it is worth noting how infrequently Paul raises the topic (1 Cor 6:9–10; cf. 1 Tim 1:9–10). In the present passage, same-sex relations are not the main issue—failure to recognize and honor God is. Paul's letters, moreover, reveal that he is much more concerned with the behaviors listed in verses 29–31.

Theological and pastoral reflection should recognize both "hands" of exegesis, while bringing other important data to bear on the issue.

11

THREE TIPS FOR LGBTQ CATHOLICS INTERPRETING SCRIPTURE

Yunuen Trujillo

I came out for the first time when I was seventeen years old. Until then I had always felt undeniably and unquestionably loved by God and my parents. As a result of my coming out, I was sent to a young adult initiation retreat with a Jovenes Group, a Spanish ministry. The theme of the retreat was "God loves you and so do we."

While the members of the youth group were caring and loving, I immediately noticed the unspoken "God loves you, *but...*" coming from some of the invited speakers and preachers. Through comments they made when they were praying aloud, it became clear to me that God had an issue with homosexuality and the Bible somehow proved it. I wasn't so sure I was loved by God after that, and a sense of shame replaced the sense of peace, so I went back into the closet. It would take me about a decade to snap out of it.

Almost twenty years later, Paulist Press published my first book, titled *LGBTQ Catholics: A Guide to Inclusive Ministry*. The book is a 101 guide for Catholics who want their parishes to be more welcoming. Among other things, the book addresses the need for inclusive ministry, tackles common myths and prejudices, offers steps to create an LGBTQ ministry, gives an overview of Catholic doctrine, and includes many stories.

More than anything, the book is an invitation and a how-to guide for parishes across the world to replicate what welcoming parishes are already doing. It also includes an invitation for biblical scholars to engage in a much-needed debate and dialogue about the "clobber passages" on homosexuality.

Who is God? Does God love us? Is God a punishing God? Did God create LGBTQ people? What does the Bible say about this topic? As LGBTQ Catholics, we often must go through long journeys of discernment to arrive at a point of peace with God. Some of us find that peace away from religious circles, while others choose to stay. For those who stay, studying the Bible is often the first point of healing.

Here I offer a few tips that can help us on our journey of healing.

BE AWARE OF SCRIPTURE INTERPRETATIONS

First, we must realize that most Catholics' understanding of the Bible comes from homilies, lay preachers, Catholic media, and family members who claim knowledge of

God and the Bible. Are those preaching about the Bible fully formed to do so? The answer varies on a case-by-case basis. Our parish religious formation programs often focus on religious formation for children, which leaves little room for questioning and discernment, and there are few widespread religious formation opportunities for adults, other than marriage formation and perhaps confirmation.

We must also remember that until the mid-twentieth century, Catholics relied almost entirely on biblical interpretation by priests who may not have been well educated in biblical criticism. And many Catholics did not read the Bible on a regular basis. It wasn't until 1943, when Pope Pius XII issued the encyclical *Divino Afflante Spiritu*,[1] that lay Catholics were encouraged to interpret the Bible themselves. And only after Vatican II were Masses celebrated in local languages.

These are relatively new developments, and all Catholics are still learning to interpret the Bible. So how do we know if we, or others, are interpreting the Bible correctly?

My first tip for interpretation is: If a particular biblical interpretation does not result in simultaneous love of God, love of self, and love of neighbor, then something is missing in that interpretation.

We must remember that the Bible is a collection of books, written by men, inspired by God, and yet still written from the cultural, historical, socioeconomic, and political context in which each writer lived. In a way, the Bible describes a long journey of faith, with all its ups and downs, with the good, the bad, the ugly, and the indifferent.

For Christians, the culmination of our journey is Jesus. In the Gospel of Matthew, Jesus tells us, "Do not think that I have come to abolish the law or the prophets; I have come

---

1. Pius XII, *Divino Afflante Spiritu* [Encyclical on Promoting Biblical Studies], September 30, 1943, https://www.vatican.va/content/pius-xii/en/encyclicals/documents/hf_p-xii_enc_30091943_divino-afflante-spiritu.html.

not to abolish but to fulfill" (Matt 5:17). Jesus reminds us that whatever the interpretations of the law and conceptions of God were at the time, the Son of God is the fulfillment of it all and the greatest commandment is to love God, our neighbors, and ourselves.

This is true today more than ever. Any interpretation or quotation that is divorced from the biblical context and from the Gospels is incomplete.

THE "CLOBBER PASSAGES" ARE NOT WRITTEN IN STONE

Second, when it comes to homosexuality and the clobber passages, nothing is written in stone. What do I mean by this? Oh, where to start?

In the chapter above by Amy-Jill Levine, one of the world's leading Jewish biblical scholars, she notes something that is almost a foreign concept in Catholic circles: the fact that in many of these passages we don't really know what the author really meant.

I say this is a foreign concept because, in Catholic circles, there's often rhetoric that uplifts the institutional Church as an all-knowing protector of the truth, which is partially but not rigidly true. As the *Catechism* reminds us, the Word of God is not written and mute, rather it is "incarnate and living."[2]

The catechism assigns the huge task—and burden—of interpreting the "incarnate and living Word" to the bishops, but it also reminds us that the interpretation must be done within "the living Tradition of the whole Church,"[3] and

2. John Paul II, *Catechism of the Catholic Church*, 2nd ed. (United States Catholic Conference, 2011), §108.

3. John Paul II, *Catechism of the Catholic Church*, §113.

that Sacred Scripture is written principally in the church's heart, rather than in documents and records. It also must be informed by the Holy Spirit.

The magisterium must be attentive to the *sensus fidelium*, as the *Catechism* describes it, for "the faithful have an instinct for the truth of the Gospel, which enables them to recognize and endorse authentic Christian doctrine and practice, and to reject what is false."

In a way, the *sensus fidelium* is informed by the lived experience of all the baptized. The bishops must interpret the Bible from the lived experience of the whole people of God, including those marginalized, and such interpretation must be open to the action of the Holy Spirit, whose manifestation in LGBTQ people's lives shows God is still speaking.

But if a large part of the magisterium is far away from the lived experience of LGBTQ Catholics and other marginalized groups, the interpretation can only be incomplete.

In addition to the lack of closeness with marginalized groups, I believe there must be greater collaboration with biblical scholars from all walks of life. In the past, scholars have been reprimanded or actively discredited by the institutional church for focusing on the clobber passages and offering alternate interpretations.

The magisterium should actively encourage and offer room for biblical scholars to debate and dialogue about the clobber passages, and they should join that process of discernment. As Levine reminds us, they might still not reach a conclusion about the original meaning of some texts, but the process itself would help the magisterium and the faithful identify some key areas for improvement.

The biggest area of improvement for the magisterium and the faithful, in my opinion, is the understanding that the word *homosexuality*, first used in biblical translations in 1946, replaced an array of words and concepts in Greek, Hebrew, and Aramaic. These words did not refer to loving, committed relationships between two consenting adults who choose to love each other for a lifetime.

The words originally used evolved over time and developed different meanings, but none of them referred to what today are called same-sex civil unions or marriage. Furthermore, even if they remotely referred to such a concept as we understand it today, they were written in a particular context and scientific understanding that is different from our modern era.

The word *homosexuality* itself, and even the most basic understanding of LGBTQ orientations and identities, has evolved over the past century. Now imagine the situation after another two thousand or four thousand years. When the American Psychiatric Association (APA) published its first edition of the *Diagnostic and Statistical Manual of Mental Disorders* (DSM) in 1952, homosexuality (and let me provide a trigger warning) was classified as a "sexual deviation" within the larger "sociopathic personality disturbance" category of personality disorders.[4]

The sexual deviation diagnosis grouped together "homosexuality, pedophilia, fetishism and sexual sadism." When homosexuality was first used in translations of the Bible, it was used in passages that described abuse of minors, forced prostitution, scenarios of abuse of power, and much more. It wasn't until 1973 that the APA removed that definition of homosexuality from the second edition of the DSM, but the damage had already been done.

Many in our church still conflate an LGBTQ identity or orientation with pedophilia, and that conflation is immoral,

---

4. Jack Drescher, "Out of DSM: Depathologizing Homosexuality," *Behavioral Sciences* 5, no. 4 (2015): 565–75, doi: 10.3390/bs5040565.

damaging, and wrong to LGBTQ people. Some in the magisterium and in our church still have a long learning journey ahead, and biblical scholars, along with the lived experience of LGBTQ people and the Holy Spirit's manifestation in our lives, should inform that journey. As LGBTQ Catholics, becoming aware of these areas of improvement and knowing that God loves us can bring some healing.

LISTEN TO AND DISCERN GOD'S VOICE

Finally, my third tip for LGBTQ Catholics reading and interpreting the Bible is to listen to God's voice in your heart and follow your conscience. This is also known as the "primacy of conscience." It's cliché, but I don't believe there's anything more important than this.

I began by telling you a little about my story. It has taken a while to be at peace with myself and, in part, I wish somebody could have saved me the ten-year struggle. Yet I regret nothing. I knew God loved me, but I did not feel unconditionally loved by my community, and I had to go through that journey to reconcile both. I am now on the other side.

The biggest tool in my journey, and the one thing for which I prayed to God during that decade, was discernment. Room for discernment is key in inclusive Catholic ministry. Each one of us LGBTQ Catholics is at a different part of our journey, and self-understanding and even our own views might change over time. Inclusive ministry should be open to all no matter what part of the journey we are in.

We should not be pressured to stay in the closet, but we can also wait to come out until it is physically, spiritually, and financially safe. We are full human beings, not children. We can discern our vocation, orientation, and identity, and should be empowered to do so. We are holy, loved, and perfect the way we are.

God loves you, and she loves unconditionally.

12

GENESIS AND OUR INALIENABLE DIGNITY

Richard J. Clifford, SJ

As the opening book in the Jewish and Christian Bible, the Book of Genesis sets the tone and sounds the themes to be developed in the books that follow. No wonder that Christians and Jews revere the book and have always looked to it for answers. But sometimes answers differ from expectations, especially when we consider the context of the verses.

The Bible is not a collection of independent verses, but it fits those pieces into a story that involves us. Consider each verse, yes, but be conscious of the story being told. This approach to Genesis is needed to appreciate God's love and generosity in creating a beautiful planet and endowing it with fascinating creatures.

It is true, of course, that the just God sends a universal flood on the wicked generation of humans in Noah's day, but then goes on to create the world anew, not altering in any way the dignity and freedom given in the original creation.

It is easy, however, to miss the goodness and worth of the creatures God created.

Unfortunately, history has shown how quickly humans decided on their own that some people were less-than and were to be shunned. Think of the history of slavery and of discrimination based on skin color or other superficial differences—and in our own day of prejudice against LGBTQ people. How different was the intent of the Genesis God who created all humans as equals and endowed them with inalienable dignity and responsibility toward the planet and its creatures.

It is worthwhile, therefore, to look again at Genesis's portrayal of the worth of human beings. A good place to begin is God's decision to create humans: "Let us make man" (Hebrew *hā'ādām*). Though "man" has often been interpreted narrowly as "an adult male," the context makes clear that the word should be translated "human beings," the less common meaning of "man" in English.

We know this is correct because the very next verse (Gen 1:27) expands on *hā'ādām*: "male and female he created them." Females were not created as an afterthought, but men and women were created together and are equal in God's sight.

There are other relevant passages in the opening chapters of Genesis that similarly enlighten and encourage us today. Two passages are particularly relevant when their context is considered: the triple charge that God gave to humans after creating them (Gen 1:26), and the phrase "image and likeness of God" (Gen 1:26–27) that is applied to them.

After creating men and women, God gave them three commands that defined them, assigning them their responsibilities and goals. "Be fruitful and multiply, and fill the earth and subdue it" and "have dominion over the fish of the sea and over the birds of the air and over every living thing that moves upon the earth" (Gen 1:28).

The three commands are linked. The first command endorses sexuality as a means for begetting the next generation, enabling the human species to continue in existence. The second command builds on the first, since human life, especially at that time, would have been impossible without adequate land to supply families with food and clothing (from locally grown flax, wool, and cotton).

Trade at the time was limited to luxury goods, and so did not include ordinary foodstuffs or clothing. Note also that the divine charge has in view humans as *grouped*, that is, families with plots of land, and nations with territories.

The third divine command goes beyond self-centered or nation-centered interests: "Have dominion over the fish of the sea and over the birds of the air and over every living thing that moves upon the earth." The verb rendered here "have dominion over" (Hebrew *rādāh*). Humans are not meant to be passive toward nature. In the context, "have dominion over" means that humans accept responsibility for the three domains of sea, sky, and earth, and see to the flourishing of the creatures in each domain.

Given the importance today of human care for the environment, this third command deserves illustration. Originally according to Genesis 1, humans were vegetarians (Gen 1:29–30) and only later, in view of their frequent recourse to violence, did God allow them to take living creatures for food (Gen 9:2–6).

One example of humans' nurturing nonhuman life will suffice. In Genesis, Noah is told what creatures to bring into the ark and save from the flood to repopulate the earth:

> Of the birds according to their kinds, and of the animals according to their kinds, of every creeping

> thing of the ground according to its kind, two of every kind shall come in to you, to keep them alive. Also take with you every kind of food that is eaten, and store it up; and it shall serve as food for you and for them. (Gen 6:20–21)

Another version of the flood story (Gen 7:2) puts the command differently: "Take with you seven pairs of all clean animals." The divine command in either version is clear: humans are responsible for preserving their natural environment and seeing to the continuation of the creatures in each domain. Humans may take what is necessary for themselves, but even when they do, they must further the divinely intended flourishing.

Though not strictly speaking a defining imperative, the phrase in Genesis 1:26–27, "in our image, according to our likeness," is exceptionally important for understanding human beings. It reads, "Then God said, 'Let us make humankind in our image, according to our likeness.'" What do "image" and "likeness" mean in this context?

"Image" and "likeness" in the Bible sometimes refers to a statue in the round; among Israel's neighbors, it commonly referred to a king or a deity whose authority was represented by the statue. The biblical meaning of the image and likeness of God is best explained by the purpose clause that immediately follows, "*and* let them have dominion over the fish of the sea...."

Genesis's use of "image" and "likeness" to describe humans' task of dominion over other creatures seems like a deliberate critique of the creation accounts of its neighbors, in which humans are portrayed as powerless slaves of the gods.

Genesis totally differs: God entrusts humans to rule over the earth. Psalm 8 even compares humans' rule over the earth to heavenly beings' (angels) rule over heaven:

Yet you have made them a little lower than God,
  and crowned them with glory and honor.
You have given them dominion over the works of your
    hands;
  you have put all things under their feet,
all sheep and oxen,
  and also the beasts of the field,
the birds of the air, and the fish of the sea,
  whatever passes along the paths of the seas.
    (Ps 8:5–8)

The image of God became an important theme of subsequent Christian theology. In the history of Christian thought, interpretation of the phrase can be classed either as *substantialist,* in which *image* refers to the human soul mirroring its divine archetype, and *functionalist,* which refers to the human task of ruling in accord with the ancient biblical and Near Eastern meaning of *image.*

The substantialist view owes much to the Platonic philosophy that influenced patristic theology. The functionalist meaning is more common today. Humans are indeed an image and likeness of God, which expresses not only their dignity and thoughtfulness, but also their authority over and responsibility for the world in which they live.

It is important that all human beings today, especially those in the LGBTQ community sidelined by misunderstanding, embrace the dignity and responsibility granted them by the Creator, and reject human judgments that exclude and diminish them.

13

THE INVITATION OF THE GOSPELS

John R. Donahue, SJ

As churches grapple with issues of sexual life and morality in a changing world and turn to the Bible for guidance, the few New Testament texts that are often discussed are the very worst places with which to start. In a recent article for *Outreach*, the Scripture scholar Walter Brueggemann calls them "texts of rigor." We will return to them later—and briefly.

First, we turn to the life and teachings of Jesus as a fundamental resource in capturing the liberating power of the gospel and unmasking the destructive force of selective interpretation.

WHO IS COMING TO DINNER?

The first follower of Jesus—after Peter, his brother Andrew, and the sons of Zebedee—is Levi, a son of Alphaeus. Christ goes to Levi's house where "many tax collectors and sinners were also sitting with Jesus and his disciples—for there were many who followed him" (Mark 2:15). Scribes and Pharisees, the doyens of the religious establishment, are shocked and ask his disciples, "Why does he eat with tax collectors and sinners?" (Mark 2:16).

This question evokes a quick response from Jesus: "I have come to call not the righteous but sinners" (Mark 2:17). Jesus's presence is an invitation to a new perspective on God's presence.

Later in his ministry, after John is imprisoned, Jesus derides a generation who called John the Baptist demonic because of his ascetic and radical lifestyle (which included not eating or drinking). They blamed him—the Son of Man—for just the opposite, shouting: "Look, a glutton and a drunkard, a friend of tax collectors and sinners!" (Matt 11:19). Such was the name of Jesus before he was called "Messiah," "Lord," or "Savior."

Tax collectors at that time were not wealthy colonials who purchased the office from Roman occupiers and gleaned exorbitant profits for themselves. Rather, they were local officials responsible for a host of taxes and tolls that touched many aspects of ordinary life. Jewish temple officials also collected taxes, an added suffering on a beleaguered population. Tax collectors were often scorned because of their dishonesty and association with the Roman occupiers of the land.

The other friends of Jesus, the sinners, represent a wide spectrum of people ranging from people notorious for their immoral activities, such as thieves, prostitutes, and brawlers, to people who, by their very professions as tax collectors, peasants, or farmers, could not be expected to live a full Jewish religious life. They did not follow the Torah as it was taught by religious leaders.

Also, physical maladies were thought to be the effect of

sin and precluded full participation in community and religious life. "Rabbi, who sinned, this man or his parents, that he was born blind?" (John 9:2).

Being marginalized and considered suspect by those with whom they lived was the burden of sinners, but they were invited by Jesus: "Come to me, all you that are weary and are carrying heavy burdens, and I will give you rest.... For my yoke is easy, and my burden is light" (Matt 11:28, 30).

Later, as his disciples listen, Jesus berates the religious officials who lay heavy burdens on the shoulders of others but will not move them with a finger (Matt 23:4).

Where is Jesus found today? He is found among LGBTQ people carrying the burden of suspicion and marginalization, inflicted, all too often, by those who invoke the Bible to justify the very things that are counter to the life and teaching of the prophet from Galilee.

CROSSING BARRIERS

In his remarkable book *The Dignity of Difference*, the late Jonathan Sacks, who was for twenty-two years the chief rabbi of the United Hebrew Congregations of the British Commonwealth, unlocks the richness of the Hebrew Scriptures and the Jewish tradition "to counter the human tendency to dislike the unlike and exclude people not like us from our radius of moral concern." His fundamental insights provide a lens for reading the New Testament.

In another book, *Then the Whisper Put on Flesh: New Testament Ethics in an African American Context*, the Presbyterian theologian Brian K. Blount writes that the Gospel of Luke presents "a tableau where Jesus breaks through social and religious barriers by positioning Jesus in the continual company of social misfits...and actualizes the theme of reversal by the way he behaves."

Religion often creates hatred and suspicion of the other. These feelings are particularly acute when two groups claim to be the authentic interpreters of a shared tradition—visible in our own day in the split between Sunni and Shiite Muslims, as one of several examples. During Jesus's lifetime, a long-standing chasm existed between Jews and Samaritans.

This tension, which broke out often into warfare and violence, was especially strong during the New Testament period. During the time of the Roman prefect Coponius, when the Jews were celebrating the Festival of Unleavened Bread, some Samaritans scattered human bones in the temple, thus polluting it so that sacrifices could not be offered. After a clash between Galileans and Samaritans, the Galileans elicited the help of Eleazar, a robber, and with his assistance, plundered Samaritan villages.

This hatred between the Jews and Samaritans is reflected in the Gospels. The Samaritan woman at the well says to Jesus, "How is that you, a Jew, ask a drink of me, a woman of Samaria?" and the Johannine editor notes, "Jews do not share things in common with Samaritans" (John 4:9). The woman later testifies that the dispute involved their respective temples: "Sir, I see that you are a prophet. Our ancestors worshiped on this mountain, but you say that the place where people must worship is in Jerusalem" (4:19–20).

Later, the opponents of Jesus ask, "Are we not right in saying that you are a Samaritan and have a demon?" (John 8:48). Jews and Samaritans looked on each other as "the hated other," each of which was a threat to their respective religious and national identities.

GUIDES ALONG THE WAY

The Gospel of Luke counters this culture of hatred. Luke organizes his Gospel around a great journey narrative, where Jesus travels from Galilee in the North, through Samaria, and on to Jerusalem in the South (Luke 9—19). On his death march, Jesus speaks words of life. At the outset of his journey, he sends the disciples as messengers "ahead of him" to a village of the Samaritans "to make ready for him...but they did not receive him" (Luke 9:52–53).

In response, James and John ask Jesus if he wants them to call fire down from heaven and destroy them, but Jesus "rebukes" them, a term usually used when Jesus casts out demons (Luke 4:35, 41; 9:42). The request of James and John continues the stereotype of the evil Samaritans, while Jesus's rebuke foreshadows the reversal of attitudes toward the Samaritans that will unfold throughout the journey.

Two other Samaritan stories in Luke shatter entrenched prejudices and divisions, not only for their first hearers but for all who would claim the gospel as a guide. As Jesus continues along his journey, he is confronted by an expert in Jewish law, who wants to test him (see Luke 10:25–28).

The expert asks what he should do to inherit eternal life. Jesus answers with a question: "What is written in the law? What do you read there?" (Luke 10:26). The lawyer responds with the commands from Jewish law to love God and neighbor (Deut 6:5; Lev 19:18), and Jesus approves his answer. But continuing to test Jesus, the legal expert asks, "And who is my neighbor?" (Luke 10:29).

The legal language disappears, and Jesus tells him a parable, which shocks his understanding of neighbor and describes what it means to be a neighbor (Luke 10:30–37). The parable narrates the intersection of various personal histories. Though compact, it moves forward rapidly by engaging the reader in a series of dramatic tensions.

A traveler from Jerusalem to Jericho described simply as "a man," like the "everyman" of medieval plays, is beaten, robbed and left half dead beside the road. All identifying characteristics are gone; we don't know whether he is rich or poor, Jew or Samaritan. Then, one by one, three travelers come down the road.

The first, a priest, arrives "by chance," sees him and walks past, as does the second passerby, a Levite. Too often we interpret this as a bit of anti-Jewish polemic, but if the priest and the Levite were going to Jericho to perform religious duties, any contact with a corpse would have made them unclean. They are good people caught in a dilemma.

Next comes a Samaritan. Given the intense hatred between Jews and Samaritans in Jesus's day (cf. John 4:9; 8:48), Jesus's hearers may have expected the Samaritan to finish the man off. Yet the rhythm of "seeing" and passing by is broken by the explosive Greek verb *esplanchnisthe*, meaning "moved with compassion." Only then does the Samaritan enter the world of the injured man with saving help.

He stops, tends to the wounds of the half-dead man and brings him to an inn with instructions that they care for him. Here, Luke combines "seeing" and compassion, as he does when Jesus sees and has compassion for the widow at Nain (Luke 7:13), and when the father welcomes home his prodigal son (Luke 15:20). Compassion is that divine quality that, when present in human beings, enables them to feel deeply the suffering of others, and move from the world of observer to the world of a companion with the afflicted.

Like all parables, this story has multiple meanings. Most shocking in the parable, though, is not that someone stopped. It would be a story of compassion if a Jewish layperson stopped. The parable forces us as readers to put together "good" and

"Samaritan." The outsider provides the model of love of neighbor; the apostate fulfills the law.

We might also put ourselves battered in the ditch and ask if we are ready to be helped by those we would class as outsiders. Who today teaches us and enacts for us the meaning of love of God and neighbor? The parable ends, but now Jesus is the questioner, asking the lawyer, "Which of these three...was a neighbor to the man who fell into the hands of robbers?" The lawyer grudgingly answers: "The one who showed him mercy" (Luke 10:36–37).

Biblical mercy is not forsaking punishment or forgiving wrongdoing, but simply put, "saving help." The outsider is the true neighbor.

As text, this parable is a "classic"—that is, any text, event, or person that unites particularity of origin and expression with a disclosure of meaning and truth, available in principle to all human beings. It challenges its readers (and listeners) to move beyond their social and religious constructs of good and evil. It also subverts their tendency to divide the world into insiders and outsiders.

It makes us realize that goodness may be found precisely in those we most often call marginal, or a threat to the standing moral code.

Compassion shapes another parable Jesus tells along the way. All of us have heard the story of the prodigal son, but deeper images surround this family (Luke 15:11–32). A young son asks his father for his inheritance, packs off to the wide world, joins the wrong crowd, and squanders his money. Wallowing in misery, he admits his foolishness and plans a return speech: "Father, I have sinned against heaven and before you; I am no longer worthy to be called your son; treat me like one of your hired hands" (Luke 15:18–19).

Seeing him in the distance, the father, filled with compassion, runs and kisses his son. The son gives his prepared speech, but before he cries out "treat me as one of your hired hands," the father showers him with signs of love, acceptance, and freedom, and tells everyone, in essence, "Let's party!"

But the older brother, coming home from a hard day on the farm, hears singing and dancing, and when told that his father is throwing a party for his long-lost brother, the elder son does not join the celebration. The father comes out and begs him to join, saying his brother has returned safe and sound. But the older brother angrily says, "Listen! For all these years I have been working like a slave for you, and I have never disobeyed your command; yet you have never given me even a young goat so that I might celebrate with my friends" (Luke 15:29).

Again, the father pleads, reminding him that his brother "was lost and has been found" (Luke 15:32). The parable doesn't tell us whether the elder son joined the party.

The attitudes of the two sons are key to the deeper meaning of the parable. The younger son thinks that the way to return to the father's good graces is to be treated as a servant; the older one boasts that all these years he has been a dutiful servant. Both define sonship in terms of servile obligations, and each, in his own way, destroys the family.

The story is really a tale of the "prodigal father"—a man lavish in his love, who shatters the self-understanding of both sons and wants both to be free. In the parable, the love of the father reaches out to both the wayward and the dutiful.

A SURPRISING "FOREIGNER"

While the Good Samaritan is the prime example of the teaching of Jesus breaking through religious and social barriers, for its full import we must reflect on the third Samaritan story, the healing of the ten lepers (Luke 17:11–19).

Placed near the end of Jesus's journey to Jerusalem, on the edge of Samaritan territory, ten people afflicted with the horror of leprosy (some skin disease that made them "unclean") cry out from a distance: "Jesus, Master, have mercy on us" (Luke 17:13).

According to the law, they are to remain at a distance (cf. Num 5:3) and to shout to warn people of their presence (cf. Lev 13:45–46). Jesus's healing response is immediate, and he directs them to go to the priests who will authenticate the cure. Leviticus 13–14 contain over a hundred verses with elaborate descriptions of the treatment of diseases and criteria for their cure.

But Luke's narrative moves beyond a standard healing narrative when one of the lepers returns "praising God with a loud voice" (Luke 17:15) and prostrates himself before Jesus. Surprised, Jesus wonders why only one of the ten has returned and given thanks. The Gospel notes that he is a Samaritan, whom Jesus calls "a foreigner" (17:18). (The Greek literally means "a person of a different kind or nature.")

Throughout Luke's Gospel, "praising God" is a fundamental response to the presence of God in the actions of Jesus (see Luke 2:14, 20; 19:38; 23:47). In these significant places, those who give such glory are people on the margins of Jesus's society. Shepherds (along with tax collectors) are listed among those occupations that no observant Jew should pursue. Samaritans were hated and suspect, and a leper who was a Samaritan was doubly scorned, both for his disease and for his religious and ethnic identity.

A Gentile centurion, who is also of a different kind as well as a representative of an occupying power, glorifies God and calls Jesus "innocent" (Luke 23:47). The actions of the Samaritan in the parable and of the Samaritan leper comprise two religious attitudes that are fundamental to both Judaism and the teaching of Jesus.

Jewish teachers in the first century defined the two fundamental religious actions as worship of God and love of neighbor. The Samaritan leper who twice gives glory to God embodies the first of these fundamental dispositions, while the good Samaritan is a model of love of God expressed in love of neighbor. Luke forcefully says that those who are called enemy and scorned as outsiders are fulfilling fundamental religious attitudes expected of both Jews and all followers of Jesus.

Martin Luther called the parable of the prodigal son the "Gospel within the Gospel." Perhaps, for our day, these Samaritan narratives should be called the Gospel within the Gospel.

BAD NEWS IN THE BIBLE?

I mentioned earlier that I would not then deal with what Walter Brueggemann has called "texts of rigor." Those texts are constantly invoked to pillory LGBTQ people and exclude them from aspects of church life. Such texts offer little help from the New Testament when discussing issues of sexuality in the contemporary world. Lists describe actions, not dispositions, and none of these texts know of loving and free adult relationships.

The texts of rigor condemn sexual activity between men in a catalog of the corruption and wickedness of the pagan world, renouncing idolatry, envy, murder, rebellion against one's parents, slander, gossip, fornication, sodomy, thievery, slave trading, and greedy lying (see Rom 1:26–32; 1 Cor 9–11).

Certain considerations should guide any evaluation of these texts. First, they describe a world Paul's followers have left behind when they now experience freedom and new life, as they were "sanctified" and "justified in the name of the Lord Jesus Christ" (1 Cor 6:11). Second, the sexual relations so mocked were most often abusive through an imbalance of power (for example, a slave master with a servant; older men molesting young boys).

Since many of Paul's followers were former slaves who were victims of sexual exploitation, these texts proclaim that, in Christ, there is "no longer Jew or Greek, there is no longer slave or free, there is no longer male and female; for all of you are one in Christ Jesus" (Gal 3:28).

THE GIFTS AND POWER OF LGBTQ PEOPLE

We have spent time together thinking about powerful stories of the actions and words of Jesus of Nazareth. Jesus meets people where they are, shares meals with them, and talks of their love of God and neighbor. Tax collectors, sinners, Samaritans—they went through life disinherited and marginalized by the world around them.

Ordinary people avoided them, and many religious leaders shunned them. In defending and associating with them, Jesus came into conflict with those who held power. Clerical circles and civil authorities collaborated to put him on trial. He was sentenced to death. Yet the paradox of this death is that it was, and remains, life-giving.

But there are other stories that awaken hope in people today. Amid the tapestry of my early years, two decades before the Second Vatican Council, were threads of racism, religious prejudice, and the distorted norms of affective love. As the years passed, stories of people's lives once thought disturbing and the presence of friends, teachers, and guides gave way to a deeper appreciation of the beauty of human diversity.

I am now ninety-one years old. As the sands of my time run out, a recent awareness of the gifts and power of LGBTQ people join my procession of mentors. I am thinking of the kindness and generosity of a gay couple who constantly helped in accompanying a group of pilgrims on a trek through those lands where Paul of Tarsus preached about freedom from the law and the joy of the gospel.

I will always remember a student who, over thirty years ago, hesitatingly told me he was gay. After his ordination as a priest, he spent years working among the poorest of the poor, only to die of a vicious cancer at age fifty-five. He was truly one of the holiest people I've ever known. And I know parents who struggle and yet guide with love and affection a son or daughter facing their journey of gender transformation.

We should cease talking about the problem of LGBTQ people and instead be thankful for their gifts. The dignity and beauty of difference is a legacy for all those who are members of the Body of Christ.

14

SCRIPTURE AND MODERN GENDER CONTROVERSIES

Richard J. Clifford, SJ

It is understandable that Jews and Christians turn to the Bible for answers to contemporary questions. Often, they turn to the opening chapters of Genesis, which tell how God created the world and human beings in wisdom. So naturally, we look to these chapters to learn how to live fruitful and happy lives.

An example of interpreting, or rather reinterpreting, a verse in Genesis is the recent New American Bible, Revised Edition (NABRE) and the New Revised Standard Version, Updated Edition (NRSVUE) revisions of Genesis 1:26: "Let us make man" (Hebrew *hā'ādām*). The NABRE renders it "human beings" and NRSVUE, "humans." The translators reexamined the verse drawing on ancient parallel texts and pointed out, quite correctly, that "man" in this verse refers not to an individual male (the most common meaning of "man" in English), but to humankind, a less common meaning in English.

Recently, another controversy has sent readers to the creation accounts in Genesis. This controversy is not about inclusive language, as in 1:26, but about the phrase that follows in Genesis 1:27: "Male and female he created them." Why the fresh interest? Because many people, especially among the young, assert that their gender identity does not correspond with the sex registered for them at birth, and they now seek to act in accord with their actual gender identity.

This worries people who believe that such claims go against the plain meaning of Genesis 1:27. In their interpretation, the phrase is a scriptural warrant for two genders only. God established two genders in the moment of creation, and that divine act remains in force today.

But does the phrase in Genesis 1:27 negate the claims of trans people cited above? Does it even say anything about the issue? Here is the full verse in the NRSVUE: "So God created humans in his image, in the image of God he created them; male and female he created them."

The first duty is to determine the context of the verse. Outside of its context, the wording alone might seem to support the claim that God endowed humanity with only two genders: male and female. Yet this verse should not be interpreted apart from its context; it is part of a carefully crafted creation account in which each verse gains meaning from the whole account.

For much of the Old Testament, interpreters have to infer the context from the text itself. What does the entire creation story in Genesis 1 tell us about its context and purpose? The chapter opens the Bible by showing us God at work; in this case, God's unhurried and masterful arrangement of the dark and inert primordial mass into a harmonious world suitable for human habitation.

The text suggests its purpose was meant to reassure a devastated community that their Creator overcame chaos and stillness and ensured that animate beings of all kinds (including humans) would continue despite the serious threat of extinction. The text depicts a powerful deity intent on safeguarding and furthering threatened life.

Other writings of the period describe how the community struggled to believe in a God who would save them from extinction. Psalm 115, for example, asks God in anguish,

> Why should the nations say,
> "Where is their God?"
> Our God is in the heavens;
> he does whatever he pleases. (Ps 115:2–3)

Genesis 1 responds to the community's doubts about their future by showing how God arranged that all animate beings would continue through their offspring. The text does this, in a strikingly original way, by affirming that God implanted in every living creature a seed (Hebrew *zera'*) from which future generations will come. The word *seed* appears six times in the text, all of which referring to plant and animal life in Genesis 1.

For humans, however, the text uses an alternate expression to make the same point—"male and female he created them." "Male and female" thus means that humans, by divine will, share the life-potency of other life forms on earth. God's generous commitment to support human life is the proper context for interpreting "male and female he created them."

In its context, this phrase means that human beings have the same "seed mechanism" that assures that they will continue by begetting descendants to replace the generations that have gone before. Genesis 1:27 assures every human being, not only Israel, that God has implanted in them the means for continuing the future existence of humanity.

The expectation that this single verse in Genesis can adjudicate modern controversies about gender is thoroughly misguided. There is no hint that the ancient author knew anything about the modern issue of gender identity. And the text gives no hint either. To use "male and female he created them" against (or for) contemporary discussions of gender is to read *into* the biblical text rather than read the biblical text.

15

ZACCHAEUS, THE GRUMBLERS, AND LGBTQ PEOPLE

James Martin, SJ

Of all the Gospel passages that I have found helpful in ministry with LGBTQ people, the beautiful story of Zacchaeus has been the most meaningful for me (Luke 19:1–10).

At first glance, the story of Jesus's encounter with the tax collector in Jericho would seem to have little to do with LGBTQ people today. But if you read it carefully, this passage from Luke's Gospel, a masterpiece of storytelling, has a great deal to say about all those who find themselves marginalized.

Now I don't want to imply that LGBTQ people are always and everywhere "marginalized." But it's fair to say that in the Catholic Church many of them feel that way. So, as we read the Gospel, I would like to invite you to see Zacchaeus as an emblem of the LGBTQ person. Notice all the subtle resonances in the story.

To begin with, Luke tells us that Zacchaeus is the "chief tax collector" in Jericho. Now, that would have meant that he was probably "on the outs" with most of the people in this predominantly Jewish town, not only because he was colluding with the Roman authorities, but also because tax collectors had the reputation of skimming money off the top.

My former New Testament professor Daniel J. Harrington, SJ, used to say that when we read "chief tax collector" here, we should think "chief sinner." But by using Zacchaeus as a way of seeing the LGBTQ person, I'm not saying LGBTQ people are any more sinful than anyone else—we're all sinners in one way or another. Rather, they often feel "on the outs," especially in the church—like Zacchaeus probably did in Jericho.

At the beginning of the story, Zacchaeus is described as "short in stature." Luke means that he was physically small. But how little "stature" do LGBTQ people have in the Catholic Church today? They are often ignored, excluded, not listened to. And, says Luke, Zacchaeus couldn't see Jesus "on account of the crowd." Again, that means that he couldn't see over their heads, but how often does "the crowd" get in the way of LGBTQ people encountering God? How often are we part of "the crowd" that prevents people with "little stature" from coming to know God? How often is the church part of "the crowd"?

So, what does Zacchaeus do? He climbs a sycamore tree. (The homey touch of identifying the precise type of tree gives this story an added sense of historicity.) Why does he climb a tree? Because he wanted to "see Jesus." (The Greek is even more moving: he wanted "to see who Jesus was.") That's what LGBTQ Catholics want today as well: to "see Jesus." But the crowd often gets in the way. So, they must do something extra—go out on a limb—just to see what everyone else sees.

As Jesus is passing through Jericho (with what would

probably have been a sizeable crowd, since this story comes toward the end of his public ministry), he spies the diminutive tax collector perched high in the sycamore tree. Jesus invites himself to the man's house—a public sign of welcome. "Zacchaeus," says Jesus, "hurry and come down, for I must stay at your house today." Jesus is offering him what New Testament scholars call "table fellowship," an essential part of his public ministry, and something that often landed Jesus in trouble with some religious authorities.

Then comes my favorite line in the story: "All who saw it began to grumble." The Greek word used here is *panta,* all, which would have included the disciples as well. *All* began to grumble. Why? Because showing mercy to those on the margins always infuriates some people. It did in Jesus's time, and it does in ours.

So the next time you see someone opposing mercy to LGBTQ people, remember this line: they began to grumble. Why should we be surprised by it?

But that does not deter Zacchaeus at all. He shinnies down the tree and "stands there" (the Greek word used has the implication of "standing one's ground"). And he receives Jesus "with joy." Of course! How joyful it is to be welcomed into the community after probably years of feeling excluded! Many LGBTQ people know the deep joy of finally feeling welcomed, whether by their families, their friends, and even their churches.

Then Zacchaeus makes a public declaration: if he has defrauded anyone, he will repay them four times over and he will give half his money to the poor. This is usually considered to be Zacchaeus's conversion from whatever sins he committed. And indeed, in the Gospels, any encounter with Jesus provokes a conversion. (By the way, I'm not alluding to "conversion therapy," but rather to *metanoia,* the word Jesus used for the thoroughgoing change of mind and heart that we are all called to.)

But recently, I discovered something surprising about this gospel passage. The English translation that we use at Mass, from the New Revised Standard Version, is: "Half of my possessions, Lord, I will give to the poor." But the Greek is in the *present tense*: "I give (or am giving) half of my possessions to the poor." Zacchaeus seems to be *already* doing that. In other words, the conversion that is occurring may be not only Zacchaeus's conversion, but the *crowd's* conversion as well, as Jesus reveals to them that the one who was on the "outside" is more generous than they had ever imagined. How often is that the case with LGBTQ people, after people in the church come to know them!

At the end of the story, Jesus calls Zacchaeus a "son of Abraham" (Luke 19:9). It's a phrase that would have resonated deeply with the Jewish crowd. Earlier in Luke's Gospel, Jesus called the woman who was "bent over" the "daughter of Abraham" after he has healed her (Luke 13:16). In both cases, Jesus is reminding the crowd that "they" are part of "us."

In this beautiful Gospel narrative, Jesus has demonstrated his inclusion of Zacchaeus not only by inviting himself to dine at his house, but by using the phrase "son of Abraham," which tells the crowd explicitly, "This man is one of us."

So it seems that there are two places we can stand regarding ministry to LGBTQ people, and indeed to any who feel on the margins. You can stand with the crowd who "grumbles"—or you can stand with Jesus.

16

JESUS'S HEALING OF GENTILES

Brian McDermott, SJ

There's a moment in Mark's Gospel (Mark 7:31–37) when Jesus travels to Gentile territory, that is, outside of Jewish territory, to the people many Jews would have considered objects of contempt (and vice versa). He had just healed the daughter of a Syro-Phoenician woman, a Gentile. Now, he responds to a request from a group of Gentiles to heal a friend of theirs. The man is deaf and has a speech impediment. He can't make himself understood when he speaks.

Jesus responds to the group's request by acting almost like a Hellenistic wonderworker. He puts his fingers into the man's ears and some of his spittle on the man's tongue and says a "foreign" word—foreign at least to his Greek-speaking readers—the Aramaic word for "be opened" (Mark 7:34). But what Jesus is doing is not magic. He looks up to heaven, asking for divine power to show itself, and then issues an authoritative command. Jesus's word heals the man so that he now hears and speaks in a way that allows people to understand him.

In this passage and in the one about the Syro-Phoenician woman (see Mark 7:24–29), Mark wants us to recognize that Jesus's mission is not only to his fellow Jews but to the Gentiles as well.

Commentators note that the Greek expression used here to describe how Jesus heals the man, which translates to "his tongue was released" (Mark 7:35), suggests that Jesus is liberating the man from demonic power. The language Mark uses here implicitly refers to passages in Isaiah that use similar vocabulary to speak about the future time when God will fulfill God's promises to Israel. Mark wants his readers to appreciate the fact that Jesus's healing of the deaf and the mute is a sign of that promised in-breaking reign of God, the arrival of the Messiah.

I believe that this Markan text can help us in our time. It offers lessons that we Christians may use to approach LGBTQ issues and people with deepening respect and love, on the model of Christ.

We are living in extraordinary times, a time of epochal change. We all could recite a huge list of things that are wrong with our times, but there are also extraordinary advances being made.

Some sixty years ago, we witnessed the emergence of the gay rights movement. And more recently, we have witnessed transgender people coming into the light from the shadows. These folks weren't listened to, to put it mildly, and society's prejudice and hatred made it impossible for them to speak openly in a way that would allow other folks to understand them.

But we are now in the situation where LGBTQ people are articulating who and what they are and asking for recognition and respect.

Is it a stretch to relate these movements to what Jesus was doing in his time with the despised Gentiles? Is it a stretch to perceive the action of the Holy Spirit in people who are naming who and what they are to those of us who, up until now, saw ourselves as the undisputed norm for human identity? Everything in this arena is relatively new, and those who are thoroughly shaped by the traditional understanding of human sexual identity find this emergence not only challenging but scary.

Jesus tells us in John's Gospel that the Holy Spirit, the divine Advocate, will lead us into all truth if we listen to that Spirit and follow its inspirations (John 16:13). Here, Jesus is referring principally to our coming more and more into the truth of Jesus as the definitive self-revelation of God, of the Creator of all, whom he called "Abba." But could it also be the case that the Spirit is leading us to more and more truth about the images of God in our midst, human beings, in all their God-given diversity?

For many centuries, most human beings in many areas of the world have forced people different from them to live in the shadows, on the margins of society, with terrible feelings of shame and guilt. These minorities have been on the receiving end of horrifically hateful speech and actions.

But in our time, we are being asked by these people to meet them with respect and love as they emerge from the shadows—to treat them as fellow images and children of God. And we need to accept the fact—the truth—of the existence of these people. They are not going away. They are here to stay—part of God's family, which is all of humankind.

Christians who are deeply troubled by the emergence of these people of varied sexual identity and sexual orientation need to ask for the grace to live out, in wider fashion, the commandment to love their neighbor as themselves. The risen Jesus, working through the Holy Spirit, wants to heal our hearing so that we can listen actively and deeply to those who differ from us. And the Spirit wants to loosen our tongues to speak to these folks with truth and love and to speak about them to others with truth and love.

I'm not saying anything strange or far-fetched here. But we are not all living out the love commandment in this area. The whole people of God—lay members, lay ministers, deacons, priests, and bishops—are called to live the love commandment and model that behavior to others. (Remember that in the New Testament, love is not a matter of warm feelings about others; it is a way of life that seeks to increase the authentic flourishing of the other.)

The risen Jesus, working through the Holy Spirit, wants to heal our hearing so that we can listen actively and deeply to those who differ from us. And the Spirit wants to loosen our tongues to speak to these folks with truth and love, and to speak about them to others with truth and love.

As Christians, we are called to some specific activities.

First, we must seek the best scientific understanding of LGBTQ issues. Here, it is important that we distinguish between solid science that is faithful to its methodologies and ideology posing as science.

Second, we need to avoid using scriptural texts as proof texts, taken out of context and ignoring the literary form that is being used. Let's stop citing "male and female [God] created them" (Gen 1:27) as if this bit of Scripture is dealing with our contemporary issues! We need to determine theologically what divine revelation tells us about human sexuality and what it does not intend to tell us.

Third, we are called to listen deeply to these fellow human beings and to seek to understand their experience from their perspective.

And lastly, we are called to pray to the Holy Spirit to lead us Christians to the truth: the scientific truth and the revelatory truth concerning human sexual identity and sexual orientation. This kind of prayer requires that we pray for the gift of freedom from all biases, and for the ability to listen well to the data and to the persons who might differ from us, and to engage them with compassion, understanding, and love.

In the West, we live in an unprecedented time, as people who have dwelled in the shadows because of their sexual identity find their voice and ask us, at long last, to understand them and to appreciate them. These practices will help us to become a patient people, discovering what God wishes us to unlearn and discovering what new learning God desires for us.

LIST OF CONTRIBUTORS

Harold W. Attridge is a New Testament scholar and retired professor at Yale Divinity School, where he was dean from 2002 to 2012. A former president of the Catholic Biblical Association, he has authored or edited over twenty books since 1981.

Walter Brueggemann was one of the world's leading Old Testament scholars and the author of nearly one hundred and fifty books. From 1986 to 2003, he was the William Marcellus McPheeters Professor of Old Testament at the Columbia Theological Seminary in Decatur, Georgia.

Richard J. Clifford, SJ, a leading Old Testament scholar, is the founding dean of the Boston College School of Theology and Ministry and the former dean of the Weston Jesuit School of Theology, from 1983 to 1987. A past president of the Catholic Biblical Association, he began teaching at the former Weston College in 1964 and retired from Boston College in 2023.

John R. Donahue, SJ, was a renowned New Testament scholar. He taught for many years at the Jesuit School of Theology at Berkeley, served as president of the Catholic Biblical Association, and is the author of many books on the Bible, including *The Gospel in Parable*. He is also the coeditor, with Daniel J. Harrington, SJ, of the Sacra Pagina commentary on the Gospel of Mark.

Grant Hartley is an MDiv student at Aquinas Institute of Theology in St. Louis, Missouri. He is a frequent speaker on topics such as LGBTQ+ spirituality, inculturation, and history, and has cohosted the *Life on Side B* podcast, facilitating conversations among LGBTQ+ Christians. His thoughts have appeared in outlets such as *America Magazine, Religion News Service,* and *Our Sunday Visitor News.*

Elizabeth A. Johnson, CSJ, is Distinguished Professor Emerita of Theology at Fordham University, past president of the Catholic Theological Society of America, and the author of several books, including *She Who Is: The Mystery of God in Feminist Theological Discourse*. She earned a PhD in theology from The Catholic University of America and has been awarded numerous honorary doctorates.

Amy-Jill Levine, one of the world's leading biblical scholars, is the Rabbi Stanley M. Kessler Distinguished Professor of New Testament and Jewish Studies at Hartford International University for Religion and Peace, and University Professor of New Testament and Jewish Studies Emerita at Vanderbilt University. Her publications include *The Misunderstood Jew: The Church and the Scandal of the Jewish Jesus* and the coedited *Jewish Annotated New Testament.*

LIST OF CONTRIBUTORS

James Martin, SJ, is a Jesuit priest, editor at large of America Media, consultor to the Vatican's Dicastery for Communication, and the author of many books, including *Building a Bridge,* about LGBTQ Catholics. He is also the founder of Outreach.

Brian McDermott, SJ, is Special Assistant to the President of Georgetown University. A systematic theologian by training, he is the author of books and articles in the areas of theology, spirituality, and the relationship between spirituality and the exercise of authority and leadership in organizations. He has been a spiritual director for many years and has trained spiritual directors and those who accompany others in the Spiritual Exercises of St. Ignatius of Loyola.

Brandan Robertson is a PhD student in biblical studies at Drew University, an LGBTQ activist, and the author of several books, including *Dry Bones and Holy Wars: A Call for Social and Spiritual Renewal.* His writings have appeared in *The Washington Post, The New York Times, Politico,* and *Time* magazine.

Thomas D. Stegman, SJ, was a New Testament scholar and former dean of the Boston College School of Theology and Ministry. He earned a PhD in New Testament studies from Emory University in Atlanta and is the author of several books, including *Written for Our Instruction: Theological and Spiritual Riches in Romans.*

Yunuen Trujillo is an immigration lawyer, faith-based community organizer, and lay minister. She is a religious formation coordinator at the Catholic Ministry with Lesbian and Gay Persons in the Archdiocese of Los Angeles. She earned her J.D. from the University of La Verne in California and began the Instagram account @LGBTCatholics.

Jaime L. Waters is associate professor of Old Testament at the Boston College School of Theology and Ministry. She is the author of *What Does the Bible Say About Animals?* and *Threshing Floors in Ancient Israel: Their Ritual and Symbolic Significance*.